THE 1919 BLACK SOX SCANDAL

FRONT COVER: Shoeless Joe Jackson is hustling home and scoring against the Cleveland Indians in the middle of the 1919 pennant race. (Courtesy of Leo Bauby collection.)

COVER BACKGROUND: Normally, team pictures evoke strong memories, whether of winning or losing. The 1919 team photograph of the Chicago White Sox evokes something else, something sinister. Among the smiles and intense expressions is a mystery. Just who threw the 1919 World Series, how did they do it, and why did they risk their careers and reputations for short-term gains? And how much did Major League Baseball cover up? (Courtesy of Leo Bauby collection.)

BACK COVER: The 1901 American League champion White Sox finished the season 30 games over .500. Unfortunately, the National League refused to participate in a World Series until 1903. The White Sox posted nine winning seasons in their first decade, including a World Series win over the Cubs in 1906. Owner Charles Comiskey, proudly standing out with his bow tie and hat in the middle of the first row, would be devastated by the stigma of the 1919 scandal. (Courtesy of Leo Bauby collection.)

THE 1919 BLACK SOX SCANDAL

Dan Helpingstine

Copyright © 2019 by Dan Helpingstine
ISBN 978-1-4671-0376-3

Published by Arcadia Publishing
Charleston, South Carolina

Printed in the United States of America

Library of Congress Control Number: 2019931288

For all general information, please contact Arcadia Publishing:
Telephone 843-853-2070
Fax 843-853-0044
E-mail sales@arcadiapublishing.com
For customer service and orders:
Toll-Free 1-888-313-2665

Visit us on the Internet at www.arcadiapublishing.com

*To all baseball historians who have explored
and attempted to explain the Black Sox scandal.*

CONTENTS

Acknowledgments		6
Introduction		7
1.	Overshadowed by Controversy	11
2.	Baseball's Infamous Year	33
3.	Two Trials	47
4.	Recovery	59
5.	Dreams	81
6.	Overachieving	89
7.	Overcoming History	99
8.	Shoeless Joe Jackson	111

ACKNOWLEDGMENTS

As always, in a project such as this, a writer receives assistance from various sources to make the work complete. I would like to take this opportunity to thank the following persons who assisted in the creative process.

I begin by thanking photographer Ron Vesely and the Chicago White Sox for some of the photographs in this book. They are of great historical value, and hopefully will bring back cherished memories for White Sox fans by recalling true team highlights.

Arlene Marcley was of special help to me in providing images of and information about the Shoeless Joe Jackson Museum in Greenville, South Carolina. Joe Jackson is the most important and symbolic figure in the 1919 saga. Arlene went out of her way to help me, and she is a true baseball fan and historian.

Roman Weinberg was a gracious host at the Field of Dreams Movie Site. The site and the movie make a compelling case for the reinstatement of Joe Jackson into Major League Baseball. They also help the fan understand the tragedy of the Black Sox scandal and find forgiveness for anyone involved.

Jeff Torborg, who managed the White Sox from 1989 to 1991, was very generous in giving his time. His storytelling was entertaining, and his major-league insight was valuable.

My appreciation also goes out to collector Leo Bauby for his valued assistance in securing images and photographs for this work, which include the front and back covers and photographs not otherwise credited.

I also again very much enjoyed working with my editor and colleague at Arcadia Publishing, Caitrin Cunningham. Caitrin was a steadying and encouraging force, and I am grateful for her assistance in completing this book.

INTRODUCTION

"The story of the fix is the story of a flock of lambs who appealed to the wolf to protect him. Whatever happened thereafter was inevitable."

—Author Leo Katcher in his biography on gambling kingpin Arthur Rothstein

Many baseball historians—both dedicated fans and writers—have researched the 1919 Black Sox scandal. Books and extensive essays have been written; movies and documentaries have been produced. The history of the scandal is a living one. However, despite this detailed examination, or even because of it, the search continues for explanations and answers. Contradictions are everywhere; true closure seems to be nowhere.

One thing is very clear: The Chicago White Sox threw the 1919 World Series, or at least key players did enough to lose games to the Cincinnati Reds. The Series was not an example of the sun getting in someone's eyes, or a bad-hop grounder sneaking through the infield. Nor is it a story of an overconfident team, like the fictional hare, getting caught up in its own arrogance. White Sox pitchers Eddie Cicotte and Lefty Williams were both 20-game winners during the regular 1919 season. The pair posted a combined and amazing 52-18 record. In the World Series, they went an improbable 1-5. Catcher Ray Schalk knew something was wrong and was on the verge of attacking Williams after the second game loss. This and other evidence suggests that the better team lost due to physical threats and money changing hands, not because of a great upset.

One other thing is very clear: Parallels can be drawn from the 1919 White Sox to the current Major League Baseball franchise. In this case, history is not just something that is part of the past.

Shoeless Joe Jackson is easily the most controversial person connected to the 1919 World Series, and in some ways, is the most controversial of all major-league players. His detractors say that his World Series stats are misleading, and that his lifetime suspension was deserved. Regardless, today, Major League Baseball wants nothing to do with him, even decades after his death.

During the immediate aftermath of the scandal, sportswriters penned letters to the baseball commissioner defending Joe Jackson as a player and man. He thought winning a 1924 civil case vindicated him. Three years before he died, he got the help of a journalist to tell his story in detail and make his case of having played an honest 1919 World Series. A major feature film decried the fact that Jackson has not been reinstated into Major League Baseball and has not been elected to the Hall of Fame. His last home has now been converted into a museum honoring him. Fascination about him never stops.

Yet, Shoeless Joe Jackson still has his fierce critics. Some maintain he tried to hide behind his lack of education, and others state Jackson was smart enough to know what money was all about. On a photograph showing Jackson sliding into second base in the first game of the 1919 Series used later in this book, something was handwritten above the image. A previous owner of the photo wrote that Jackson was out, almost implying that this was an example of Jackson throwing the Series. As the caption states, Jackson is clearly safe. And there is no game one record of Jackson being out at any play at second.

No other White Sox player compared to Jackson as a hitter until Frank Thomas joined the club in 1990. In a game the author attended on May 27, 1994, Thomas showed his ability to hit to all fields by singling to center, doubling to left, and homering to right. And he did it off right-handed pitcher Mike Mussina, who came into the game with a 7-1 mark and eventually won 270 in his career. Mussina was elected into the Hall of Fame as this book was being written.

Thomas had an incredible batting eye. In 10 seasons, he drew over 100 walks and rarely swung at a bad pitch. To go along with this disciplined approach, Thomas hit for power and for average. Joe Jackson was said to have a great swing that was a model for any hitter; Thomas's powerful stroke wasn't bad, either.

However, Thomas had his critics as well. Some doubted his toughness, although twice he was accused of dogging it when it turned out that he had serious injuries. Regardless, he was not as popular as one might think considering his accomplishments. But Frank Thomas has one thing that Joe Jackson doesn't have: In 2014, he was inducted into the Baseball Hall of Fame. His place in Chicago White Sox and Major League Baseball history is assured. And in the age of steroid use, the muscular Thomas stands proven innocent and admired.

The alleged cheapness of White Sox owner Charles Comiskey has often been cited as a driving force in the Black Sox throwing the 1919 World Series. Was Comiskey really cheap? At least in some ways, no. According to baseball researchers Bob Hoie and Mike Haupert, the White Sox had one of the highest payrolls in the American League in 1919 at $88,461. The figure topped the Reds payroll by more than $10,000. Catcher Ray Schalk and second baseman Eddie Collins were the highest paid at their positions in the American League. Eddie Cicotte and Joe Jackson were near the top in their categories. However, this doesn't mean that the team as a whole was fairly compensated in comparison to the revenue they helped generate. It can also be debated if the salary structure on the White Sox team was fair. To counter these factors, Jeff Torborg, who managed the White Sox from 1989 to 1991, told the author that low pay did not justify dumping the World Series. Then he said with a laugh, he made about the same money as some 1919 players when he broke in with the Los Angeles Dodgers in 1964.

Comiskey also resisted raising ticket prices and did other things to ensure fan loyalty. In many other ways, he demonstrated his generosity. He was also described as one who truly loved the game, not as a person who would contribute to a scandal even in an unknowing way.

Another White Sox owner, current headman Jerry Reinsdorf, has also been accused by critics of being cheap. (Although technically Reinsdorf is not the owner, he is the chief executive officer who controls the financial structure of the club. He and Eddie Einhorn headed a group to purchase the team in January 1981. Reinsdorf has controlled the team longer than anyone in franchise history.) The 1994 Major League Baseball strike solidified Reinsdorf's cheapness reputation with some fans. It is believed by some that Reinsdorf was the driving force behind the 1994 work stoppage that cost the White Sox an excellent chance of appearing in the World Series. Fans wondered about Reinsdorf's priorities: profit or winning?

But what kind of boss and executive is Jerry Reinsdorf? Front office man Dave Dombrowksi was fired by team general manager Ken Harrelson in mid-1986. Here is how Dombrowski described the dismissal aftermath in a letter he wrote to the author almost 20 years ago:

> Jerry Reinsdorf was extremely supportive of me at this time and actually gave me the opportunity to re-enter the organization," Dombrowksi wrote. "However, it did not seem

the appropriate thing since my dismissal was based on philosophical differences with Ken. So, Jerry offered me the opportunity to continue to be paid by the White Sox organization until I found another job. He did not set any time limits on this even though there was no signed contract between me and the organization. He continued to carry me on the benefits the White Sox organization had and continued to help me in any way he could.

Finally, Dombrowski, whose baseball career flourished after leaving the White Sox, wrote this about the perceived cheapskate Jerry Reinsdorf: "Jerry Reinsdorf always treated me well when I worked for the White Sox organization. Most people who work for Jerry would express the same sentiments."

Another White Sox employee spoke publicly about Reinsdorf at a Society for American Baseball Research (SABR) conference held in Chicago. She spoke of her boss completely funding a trip for White Sox workers to travel to Houston to watch the 2005 World Series.

Jerry Reinsdorf is a reclusive public figure. He mistrusts the media and rarely gives interviews. The few interviews he does are structured, short, and give little indication of his overall personality. The cheapness label ties him to Charles Comiskey. However, a one-word label does not adequately describe either man in any sense. Each man had his successes and failures and is no doubt more complicated than his public image indicates. And finally, both men have one other thing in common: Comiskey built a new stadium that stood for 80 years, and Reinsdorf oversaw the construction of a new stadium that has now been the home of the White Sox for almost three decades.

The 1919 scandal, in the short and long runs, seriously impacted the White Sox as a franchise in a very immediate sense. From 1921 to 1935, the team never finished higher than fifth. The White Sox lost 102 games in 1932, the worst percentage mark in team history. Charles Comiskey would be forever embittered by feelings of betrayal and personal pain over attacks on his reputation. He died in October 1931. His team would not appear in another World Series until 1959. By then, his family had sold controlling interest of the team to a group controlled by Bill Veeck.

After the 1994 strike, the White Sox spent most of the remaining decade losing, and attendance sagged due to fan alienation. The franchise rebounded during the first decade of the 21st century, with three division titles and a world championship in 2005. The 2005 championship was the first by either Chicago baseball team in 88 years. And if there was any thought the team was cheating in 2005, it was cheating to win, not lose.

The Chicago White Sox franchise, in a historical sense, has been treated unfairly. With the rush to trash the 1919 team, an impression seemed to be made that Major League Baseball's gambling problems began and ended with the 1919 World Series. Nothing could be more untrue. Gambling and baseball long predated 1919, but the sport didn't want to address the problem for fear of affecting attendance and credibility. In fact, anyone who wanted to breach the subject was symbolically shouted down. Additionally, the 1919 scandal broke open after allegations that an otherwise meaningless August 1920 Cubs-Phillies game was fixed. The game was meaningless except for the money wagered on it. The fixing 1919 Black Sox players cannot be exonerated. Yet they also can be labeled as the Black Scapegoats.

Major League Baseball took decisive action by banning the Black Sox from ever playing the game. Almost seven decades later, it faced a similar situation over allegations that Pete Rose had bet on baseball. Rose, who has more hits than any other player in history, has also been banned for life and still has no place in the Hall of Fame. Unlike Eddie Cicotte, who had regrets, or Joe Jackson, who professed innocence, Rose has admitted his gambling and expressed no regrets. He was what he was, or so he said. How much did the baseball establishment know before the Dowd Report? Was it in denial as it was in 1919? The denial in 1919 almost led to the destruction of the sport. How close did it come with Pete Rose? With steroid use?

The 1919 Black Sox left a painful legacy. Baseball fans, even those who know there is some kind of cheating at baseball at all levels, can't come to the grips with the fact that big-league players would throw any game, especially the World Series. In connection with 1919, fans look for heroes: Joe Jackson, Charles Comiskey, some guy with "Mountain" as a middle name. Yet, in the search for heroes, it seems as if everyone begins looking like a villain. One hundred years later, the 1919 scandal still hovers over the Chicago White Sox and Major League Baseball.

Anyone who had a connection to this scandal, whether victim, bystander, or perpetrator, ended up with never-ending feelings of bitterness and betrayal. One of the gamblers eventually was shot to death after he refused to pay a gambling IOU. (He claimed he did this on principal because a poker game had been fixed.) However, this book shows there have been some instances of recovery and redemption as the White Sox overcame adversity and a haunting history. The 1920s was a terrible decade for the franchise. Maybe the 2020s, with the team's rebuilding, will be vastly different now that the Black Sox scandal has turned past the century mark. History remains, but maybe a more hopeful history can be made. And maybe fans can come to accept something that should never have happened but inevitably did.

OVERSHADOWED BY CONTROVERSY

A key scene in the 1988 feature film *Eight Men Out* occurs when actor Clifton James smugly plays White Sox owner Charles Comiskey. The Comiskey character, with a nasty grin, tells Eddie Cicotte that he, Cicotte, was not entitled to a $10,000 bonus because he had won 29, not 30 games. Cicotte supposedly felt cheated because Comiskey had Cicotte "benched" so he wouldn't have a chance to reach the 30-win plateau. This mistreatment at the hands of Comiskey was said to be the catalyst for Cicotte to conspire to throw the 1919 World Series.

In his book *Eight Men Out*, Eliot Asinof writes that the bonus offer was "said to have happened." But who said what, and when? In all of this author's research for this book, not one historian or writer provided any details about this arrangement. Did the offer happen during contract negotiations? Did it come directly from Comiskey or from a person in his front office? Would Comiskey actually offer a bonus that would exceed a player's annual salary? If Comiskey was that cheap, would the player take him at his word? Some claim the offer was made in 1917. The scene in the movie depicts it in 1919. The movie wasn't the only source of confusion. Just what year was it?

As far as the benching went, there is no evidence that Cicotte was benched or deprived of a chance to win 30 in either 1917 or 1919. He won 28 in 1917 and had not missed a turn in the rotation. Cicotte won No. 28 on the second-to-last game of the year. He won 29 in 1919, had a shot at No. 30, but pitched poorly, leaving the game after the seventh trailing 5-4.

Then there is Cicotte himself. In a 1965 interview with Joe Falls of the *Detroit Free Press* about four years before he died, Cicotte stated that he had attempted to live a decent life as a way to atone for 1919. He made no personal attacks on Comiskey in regards to a bonus or anything else. (Some players still lashed out at Comiskey decades after he died.) The bonus story doesn't hold up to serious scrutiny. Believing it would be one way to rationalize Cicotte's actions, but even Cicotte didn't claim that easy out. He even admitted his own financial situation provided more incentive than getting revenge on his boss.

The White Sox won 100 games in 1917, a franchise record that still stands today. At least it could be said they took that American League pennant fair and square. Or did they?

A couple years before the scandal, American League president Ban Johnson said, "There's no place in baseball for the gambler; no room in the ball park for his evil presence. The game, notwithstanding loose occasional charges, stands solely on history and its merits."

Yet an accusation surfaced nearly 10 years later that again labeled the White Sox as the Black Sox, although in a different manner. It came from banned player Swede Risberg with support from Chick Gandil.

According to Risberg, the White Sox took a collection of $45 per player to bribe Detroit Tigers players to "slough off" during double headers played in Chicago on September 2 and 3. The White Sox were only 3½ games ahead of second-place Boston. After sweeping the Tigers in both doubleheaders, that lead grew to 6½. The lead topped off at 10½ on the 21st and was a comfortable nine games at the end of the season.

In the early part of January 1927, baseball commissioner Kenesaw Mountain Landis investigated the Risberg accusation. Over 30 White Sox and Tigers players appeared before Landis and denied any fix. (Of course, if any admitted any wrongdoing, they could have been given a lifetime ban from baseball.) Regardless, Landis, happy not to speculate about another fix, dismissed the Risberg story and maintained the White Sox had won the four games legitimately. Landis acted like Ban Johnson: deny and move on.

In his book *The Original Curse*, baseball historian Sean Deveney states, "Baseball was so secretive about its gambling problem, that nearly a century later, we are only left with theories and best guesses."

Theories and best guesses adequately describe any dubious connections to the White Sox in 1917 and 1919. Their 1917 American League pennant would be tainted to a degree if Risberg's accusations were proven. Their 1919 team lives in infamy.

By the way, the 1917 White Sox won the World Series, beating the New York Giants four games to two. It would take them into the early part of the next century to win another.

The bow-tied Charles Comiskey sits with the new Chicago franchise that had just been transplanted from St. Paul, Minnesota. Comiskey played 12 years of pro ball himself and amassed a little over 1,500 hits. He was responsible, along with Ban Johnson, for organizing the American League and providing crosstown competition for the Cubs. Between 1901 and 1920 inclusive, the White Sox put together 16 winning seasons and four first-place finishes. Then came the Black Sox scandal revelations.

The 39th Street Grounds was the first arena that housed the Chicago White Sox. This image, with a large advertisement for the *Chicago Tribune* in right field, shows a game during the 1906 championship year. Typical of ballparks of that decade, the 39th Street Grounds was made of wood. Its capacity was less than 10,000.

What are these serious-looking and macho men doing holding roses? It was an opening day tradition for teams to exchange floral gifts to wish each other well for the upcoming season. The Sox player marked with the "3" is pitcher Doc White, who won 18 games that year. His battery mate, Billy Sullivan, is easily identified by his chest protector. This is a news photograph, and numbers were placed by individuals so they could be identified in the caption.

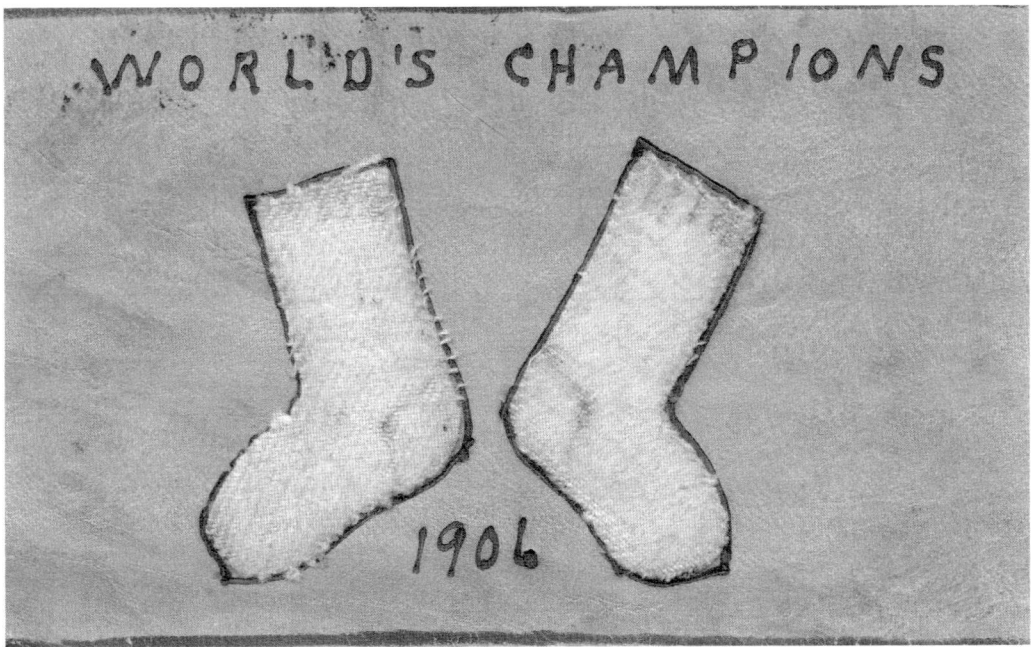

This simple image would be used in various ways over the decades as a logo for the White Sox. The 1906 World Series championship began to cement the team as a major-league franchise in Chicago. The 1906 team, known as the "Hitless Wonders," upset a Cubs team that most assumed would walk away with the championship. The year remains the only occasion when the two Chicago teams faced each other in the World Series. Both made the postseason in 2008, but each was eliminated in the division series round.

At this point, the White Sox could afford to be jovial. They were reigning world champions. Just as important, they had solidified their position as competition to the Chicago Cubs by winning the 1906 Series. After 1919, it would be a long time before the White Sox were seen with smiles like this. Presently, the team is struggling against the Cubs.

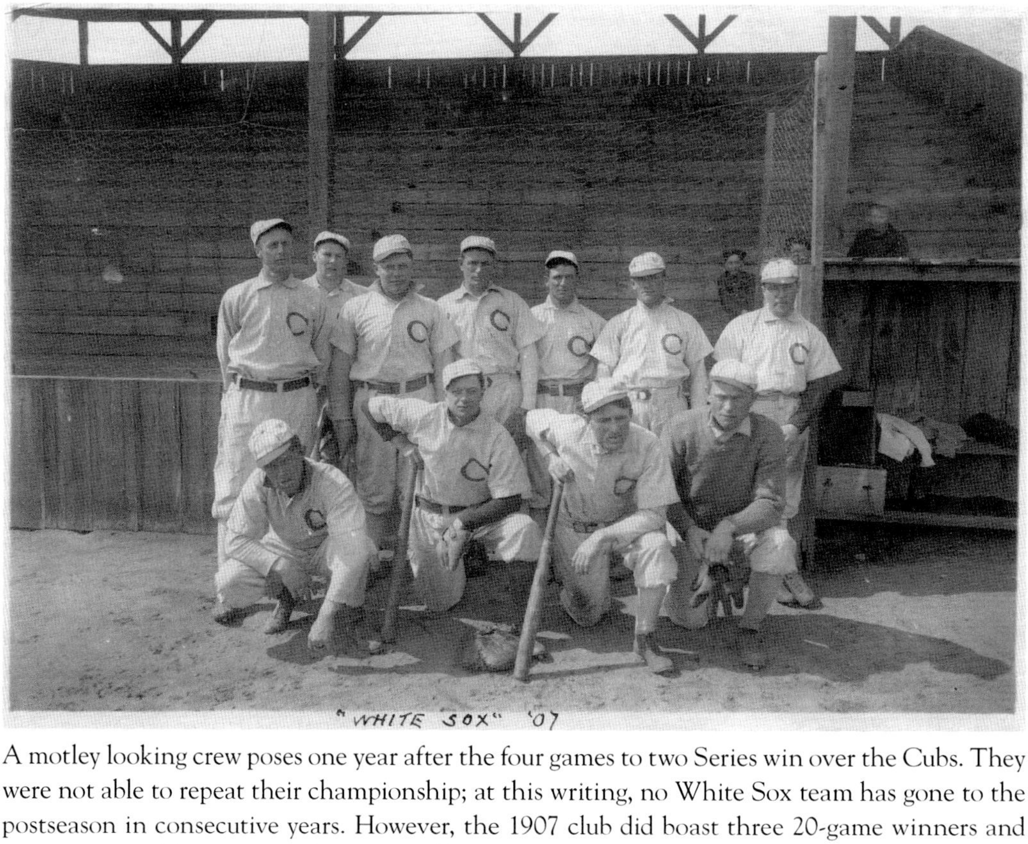

"WHITE SOX" '07

A motley looking crew poses one year after the four games to two Series win over the Cubs. They were not able to repeat their championship; at this writing, no White Sox team has gone to the postseason in consecutive years. However, the 1907 club did boast three 20-game winners and won a respectable 87 games, 5½ games off the pace. If they had repeated, they would have faced the Cubs again. From 1906 to 1908, Chicago baseball teams won three World Series. From 1909 to 2004, they captured only one. Events seemed to conspire against the White Sox and Cubs in strange ways except for the years 2005 and 2016.

This is an engraved invitation to a celebration of the winning of the 1906 World Series held the following spring. The ceremonial flag raising was held on an off day when the White Sox were on a three-day break in their 1907 schedule. These days, championships are celebrated with parades and confetti. The 1906 championship was the only time a Chicago team clinched the World Series on their home field. Ironically, the other Chicago team was the loser.

The 39th Street Grounds is shown here on an overcast-looking day. Or is that the smoke from nearby factories? This game occurred during the years just preceding the opening of Comiskey Park. As the White Sox began to win and attract larger crowds, the park could no longer accommodate all the fans. Its dimensions were 450 feet to dead center and 400 feet to the power alley in left center. It was a pitcher's ballpark, to say the least. Any success the team had until the 1970s always relied on speed and defense.

Charles Comiskey's reputation suffered due to the 1919 Black Sox as some thought he and Major League Baseball covered up the scandal. However, the park that bore his name for 80 years remains a vital part of his baseball legacy. Comiskey Park, shown here on its opening day on July 1, 1910, was a state-of-the-art structure. Made of iron and steel, Comiskey Park was viewed as much safer compared to the wooden firetrap stadiums of its day. Comiskey Park was demolished in 1991. The new stadium that opened that year still bore the Comiskey name until the franchise sold the naming rights in 2003 and it became US Cellular Field. A statue of Comiskey stands on the outfield concourse of the White Sox home field, now known as Guaranteed Rate Field.

Here is a view of Comiskey Park from behind home plate sometime during its first years. As can be seen from the center field scoreboard advertisements, beer has a historical connection to Major League Baseball. An upper deck was added to the ballpark in the late 1920s partly due to the popularity of Babe Ruth and the Yankees. The new capacity was listed at 52,000, although one crowd was announced at 55,555. That crowd attended a May 20, 1973, bat day promotion in which over 2,000 fans had to be turned away because there was no room at the inn. Fans sat on the aisle steps and stood on the scoreboard catwalk.

Until 1943, the White Sox and Cubs used to play a series for city bragging rights. This 1911 crowd appears to be jacked up for one of those games. When the two teams began playing each other again in inter-league games in 1997, crowds were more hyped than this one—sometimes nearly to the point of violence. The series has lost some of its luster, but each set of fans hates to see its team lose to their crosstown rivals. One thing can be said about the 1911 White Sox: no one could accuse the club of throwing these games. They swept the Cubs in four.

This 1912 photograph features, from left to right, right-handed pitcher Ed Walsh, Kid Gleason, and 1912 manager James Callahan. That year, Walsh won 27 games. But that paled in comparison to 1908, when Walsh won 40 (although some historians claim four wins should be scored as saves), and logged an astounding 464 innings with 42 complete games. He also made 15 relief appearances to go along with his 49 starts. Walsh has to be looked at as the greatest of all White Sox pitchers.

Eddie Cicotte is completing his wind-up during his pre–Black Sox days. Cicotte joined the team in mid-1912. He had his first breakout year with the White Sox in 1914, when he won 18 and had an ERA of 1.68.

THE 1919 BLACK SOX SCANDAL

The 1916 White Sox were beginning to take shape as a winning franchise after three consecutive losing seasons. The club finished second that year, just two games behind pennant-winning Boston. By this time, key members of the 1919 squad such as Joe Jackson, Ray Schalk, Eddie Collins, and Buck Weaver were on the roster. With this rebuilding, the team should have been on its way to real immortality. It was, but for the wrong reason.

In the early days, players worked off-season jobs not related to sports. Spring training was meant to get them back into shape in addition to preparing for the season. A couple of these players look like they dressed for colder than spring weather. Buck Weaver stands near center with a coat, and manager Clarence "Pants" Rowand is to the right wearing the same coat.

Here stand the two White Sox managers who took their teams to the World Series in the last years of the 20th century's second decade. The easily recognizable Kid Gleason is on the left, with Pants Rowand on the right. Rowand was fired after the 1918 season and probably was glad about that. Gleason stepped down after the 1923 season and never managed another major-league team. The scandal, as with most involved, weighed on him.

In this team photograph of the 1917 White Sox, Buck Weaver is lying down in a relaxed pose. The 1917 club's world championship stood as the only Chicago World Series win from 1917 until the early part of the 21st century. Yet, little is remembered about the team, as it was overshadowed by the 1919 Black Sox squad. Weaver hit .333 in the 1917 Series and scored three runs. The 1917 Sox won 100 regular-season games—the only Sox team to hit the century mark in victories.

THE 1919 BLACK SOX SCANDAL

Joe Jackson's legacy will always be haunted by controversy, but no one will ever question his picture-perfect swing. Here is his follow-through. He hit better than .300 eleven times. His lowest full-season average was .308.

Charles Comiskey was accused of being so cheap that he wouldn't pay to launder players' uniforms. This is a charge that many supporters and baseball historians deny. Here, Joe Jackson's 1917 World Series uniform looks mighty dirty. In many photographs of this time, many of the players' uniforms look like they needed a cleaning.

24   OVERSHADOWED BY CONTROVERSY

With the exception of Buck Weaver, this group of White Sox infielders doesn't look all that happy. Like the world champion Oakland A's teams of the 1970s, the 1917 White Sox were never known as a real tight bunch. Differences in education and jealousy about salaries kept members of the group from being close friends. But they could play baseball.

Oscar "Happy" Felsch stands in the middle of this 1917 White Sox outfield group. Felsch was a big RBI man for the club, but in the 1919 Series, he only hit .192 and had three driven in. The average looks anemic, although Felsch was robbed of a couple of hits by the Reds defense. He was one of the eight to be banned.

Buck Weaver always seemed to have a smile on his face. It could be in a shot like this one, in a team photograph, or even in the courthouse during the 1921 trial. Here, he is relaxing on the bench sometime during the championship season of 1917. His career ended three years later.

These 1917 White Sox infielders helped the team win the World Series only to be tainted by scandal three years later. Eddie Collins, second from the left, was the only one of this group not affected by the Black Sox fiasco. This picture is symbolic of the folly of the 1919 debacle. A talented group of major-league players turned their backs on greatness for short-term gain. The franchise never fully recovered.

This media caption describes another White Sox scandal, and is one more example of how the accomplishments of the 1917 team were overshadowed. According to Swede Risberg, White Sox players took a collection and forwarded the money to Detroit Tigers so the Tigers could "slough off" in consecutive doubleheaders played at Comiskey Park in early September 1917. Both teams denied the fix when meeting with baseball commissioner Landis in January 1927. Landis, so eager to ban the 1919 Black Sox, was happy to believe there was no scandal here. He deemed the games as legitimate with little investigation.

```
WATCH YOUR CREDIT
C 2426 "P AND A PHOTOS" CHICAGO BUREAU
   PHOTO SHOWS Swede Risberg, Eddie
Collins, Buck Weaver, and Chick Gandil.

   SHOWDOWN NEARS IN BASEBALL SCANDAL.

The quiz to be held before Commissioner
Landis on the latest scandal, the alleged
fixing of the series of 1917 between
the Chicago White Sox and Detroit Tigers
will be held Jan. 5, and an attempt will
be made to definitely settle the dust thrown
up by the accused and accusers. The above
photo, taken shortly after the alleged fixed
game, shows members of the White Sox who
are figuring prominently in the story. L to R
Swede Risberg, who started it by telling of
his collecting the money for the pool;
Eddie Collins, later manager of the team;
Buck Weaver, nationally known star, who, it
is rumored, will have something to say; and
Chick Gandil, who, from El Paso, Texas,
said that Risberg told only half of the
dirt, that every player of the Sox Team was
involved, and that he (Gandil) handed the
money to James of Detroit for division.
BFM   1-3-76
```

It is easy to tell this is the 1917 World Series by the patriotic uniform Eddie Cicotte is wearing. Cicotte won game one of the Series 2-1 with a complete game seven-hitter. He lost his next start, but threw another complete game and dropped a tough 2-0 loss. He threw everything away two years later.

THE 1919 BLACK SOX SCANDAL

Although this photograph shows fans attending the 1917 World Series, it cannot be confirmed if this is Comiskey Park in Chicago or the Polo Grounds in New York. From the wooden facade, it appears to be New York. The White Sox were shut out twice in New York in games three and four. They won game six at the Polo Grounds with the help of three Giants errors.

Along with his usual mean expression, Chick Gandil wears a patriotic uniform in 1917. In that year's World Series, he had slightly better stats than in the 1919 Series as he hit .262. Gandil picked up five RBIs in each Series. He picked up a key two-run single in the fourth inning of game six in the 1917 Series, which provided the margin in that Series-clinching win.

Dave Robertson of the New York Giants slides into third base after tripling in the fourth inning of game three at the Polo Grounds. He scored one of two Giants runs that inning, and New York won 2-0. It was a big win for the Giants, as the Sox had won the first two. Giants pitching recorded another shutout in game four, but the White Sox took games five and six and the Series.

This scene is in the Polo Grounds in New York during game six of the World Series. Eddie Collins is caught in a rundown off third after Giants pitcher Rube Benton threw to third baseman Heine Zimmermann. Zimmerman chased Collins back toward home before tossing to catcher Bill Rariden. Rariden returned the throw to Zimmerman as Rariden ran Collins to third. Collins then scored because no one was covering home and Zimmermann could not catch him. The play was set up by two Giants errors that put Collins and Jackson on base. The White Sox would score three in the inning, and that provided the difference in the win that clinched the Series. If a team wanted to throw a Series, it could have a play and an inning like this.

This is the end of the botched rundown play allowing Eddie Collins to score a key run in the Series—clinching the win for the White Sox. Either pitcher Rube Benton or first baseman Walter Holke should have been covering home.

Baseball's Infamous Year

There have been great World Series teams.

The 1927 Yankees had 60-homer-hitting Babe Ruth, won 110 games, and possessed a run differential of plus-376. Unsurprisingly, they won the World Series by sweeping the Pittsburgh Pirates and outscoring them by a 23-10 margin.

The 1968 Detroit Tigers had 30-game-winner Denny McLain (the last pitcher to win 30 in a season) and came back from a three games to one deficit to defeat defending champion St. Louis. Lefty Mickey Lolich won three games in the Series, having pitched game seven on two days' rest.

The 1976 Cincinnati Reds won their second straight Series by sweeping the Yankees. During the 1970s, the Reds appeared in two other World Series and won two other division titles. Their 1976 team has to be looked upon as the best in franchise history, far better than the 1919 squad that won a World Series it shouldn't have only because some members of the other team conspired to let them.

Then consider the 1919 Chicago White Sox.

Going into the 1919 Series, the White Sox were looked upon by many as the best team in the major leagues. A balanced club, the team had strong pitching and hitting and a solid defense. They had Shoeless Joe. They had 29-game-winner Eddie Cicotte. They had slick fielding Buck Weaver at third. Having won the World Series just two years earlier, the White Sox looked to make baseball history.

They made history all right.

The atmosphere around the Series as it began in Cincinnati was on the seemly side. The gambling maggots seemed to be everywhere, and rumors were rampant. Was this World Series on the level? Would either team ever think of throwing it? Could it be thrown?

Baseball historian Sean Deveney makes the case that one World Series had already been thrown. In his book *The Original Curse*, Deveney presents circumstantial evidence that suggests the Cubs purposely lost to Babe Ruth and the Boston Red Sox in 1918. Deveney doesn't say how much money was involved or who financed this alleged crooked scheme. He does show, however, that players from both teams were angered by a diminishing World Series share and felt economically squeezed. Motive was there, and players had threatened a strike that would have ended the Series altogether. Regardless, Deveney believes that 1919 was not the first crooked Series, and the 1918 Series may have inspired some White Sox players to take the same plunge.

Any theory by Deveney (who believed that baseball economics created an even bigger incentive to throw a Series in 1918 than in 1919) just adds to the mix as fans still try to make sense of the

THE 1919 BLACK SOX SCANDAL

Black Sox scandal. Many cannot wrap their heads around the idea that major-league players would do something like this and continue to look for explanations to rationalize this chapter of baseball history. Instead, they find contradictions and a disillusionment that has lasted a century.

One thing can be said about the after-effects of 1919: just about anyone touched by the scandal would be haunted for the rest of his or her life. Charles Comiskey, one of the men instrumental in establishing the American League, aged terribly during the 1920s. He was accused of mistreating his players and of trying to cover up the scandal to protect his team. He was forced to relive the scandal when one of his players sued him for back pay in 1924. A once great baseball franchise lay in ruins. According to Comiskey biographer Tim Hornbaker, Comiskey became reclusive and left the day-to-day management of his franchise to the front office after the scandal broke.

Joe Jackson proclaimed his innocence but was called a liar and a perjurer. Detractors claimed that his illiteracy was not a sign of stupidity and that he played the role of a dupe when he knew exactly what he was doing. Buck Weaver wanted to be tried separately from the rest but was tied to the fix and was also banned from baseball, even though there is little evidence that he threw any games or took money from gamblers. Others still lashed out at Comiskey for his cheapness, but this didn't exonerate anyone in any historical sense.

In 1919, baseball had regained its popularity with the end of World War I. Attendance was up; money was being made. The Chicago White Sox should have crowned a successful season with a world championship and perhaps should have had a string of championships. Instead, they left a black mark on baseball that has not been washed away 100 years later.

The team picture of the 1919 White Sox makes them look like a happy group. In reality, the club had internal squabbles, jealousies, and a bitterness toward its owner. For the last half of the second decade of the 20th century, the White Sox were one of the elite teams in the American League and were on the verge of another World Series appearance in 1920. Then a grand jury was impaneled. A few years later, they were feeding on the bottom of the standings.

The Cincinnati Reds, the 1919 World Series winners, also felt scarred by the Black Sox scandal. The Reds felt their championship was legitimate and that they were the better team. Center fielder Edd Roush said during the 1920 grand jury testimony, "I can't yet see how they could play the way they did and throw games. It is a mystery to me." Teammate Heine Groh added that Sox hurler Ed Cicotte gave him all he could handle. But author Eliot Asinof wrote, "Cincinnati had won its first World Series after 43 years of professional baseball—only to find it was damaged goods."

Joe Jackson doesn't look like he is dogging it here. Jackson is scoring against Cleveland during a regular season contest in late 1919. The Indians had made a run at the White Sox but ended up 3½ games out. Strangely, when the White Sox finally won their next pennant in 1959, they clinched it in Cleveland, although that stadium looked much different than this one.

Chick Gandil takes a healthy cut during 1918 spring training. That year, the White Sox slumped to 10 games under .500 in a shortened season. It was their first losing season since 1910. The team rebounded in 1919, only to throw things away.

BASEBALL'S INFAMOUS YEAR

Kid Gleason, manager of the 1919 White Sox, was described as tough and determined and a great baseball man. He had deep suspicions about his team in the early goings of the Series, to the point he was ready to choke first baseman Chick Gandil after a loss. Gleason felt betrayed by players he thought he had helped become front-line major leaguers. Although owner Charles Comiskey wanted him to remain, Gleason resigned his manager's position after the 1923 season.

This photograph was labeled by someone as "Jackson out at 1st game 1919." During the first game of the 1919 World Series, there was only one play involving Jackson at second base. This image actually shows that Jackson is safe as the Reds infielder doesn't appear to have possession of the ball. Since Jackson is the most polarizing member of the Black Sox, there is a great deal of anger directed toward him even in the present day. The person who wrote this caption may have been trying to reinforce the idea that Jackson was guilty of throwing the World Series. However, in this game, Jackson scored the lone White Sox run.

Chick Gandil is caught stealing in the second inning of the first game of the 1919 Series. If Gandil did something to throw this game, it wasn't demonstrated in the box score. Gandil went two for four and drove in the only White Sox run that day. In game three, he drove in two of the Sox three runs in a 3-0 win. In game six, Gandil batted in the winning run during the 10th inning in a 5-4 Sox victory. However, these heroics do not prove his innocence.

Here is the cropped, published version of a pre–game one image in which Jackson (left) and Cicotte are supposed to be talking to a fan by the stands. Obviously, the "fan" is not in the picture. Why he is not shown is not known and only opens things to speculation. The picture is strange, as it appears that Jackson is reaching to someone who is not there.

The original, uncropped photograph was not published in 1919. It is seen by some as a scathing indictment of Shoeless Joe Jackson. There he stands, with Eddie Cicotte and a third man in a straw hat. The third man is labeled "a fan" although some think the "fan" is actually one of the gambling conspirators. It does appear suspicious, although the "fan" has not been identified and his attendance at the park that day does not conclusively prove a connection to the scandal.

Eddie Cicotte is preparing for one of his 1919 World Series starts. Some Cicotte apologists claim he didn't throw 1919 World Series games. Instead, they claim a sore arm hampered his performance. Cicotte did have arm problems in 1918 and 1919, and he was rested some in 1919 as a result. But there are many ways a player can help throw a game: not lay down a bunt, not turn a double play, miss a cut-off man. In Cicotte's case, in the fifth inning of game four at Chicago, he cut off and then mishandled a throw heading to the plate. In that loss, Cicotte threw a complete-game five-hitter, which suggests his arm wasn't bothering him. There are many ways to throw a game, some of which are pretty easy and can go undetected.

If anyone squandered his career, it was Claude "Lefty" Williams. He won 23 in 1919 and followed that with 22 more wins in 1920. Williams started the last game of the 1919 Series. If the Sox had won that game, they might have pulled out a Series win in game nine. Williams claimed that he wanted to win that game, but feared violent reprisals to him and his family from the gamblers. He didn't make it out of the first inning in a 10-5 loss. Some don't believe the story about the threats. At the time of his suspension in 1920, Williams had an 82-48 lifetime record and a great baseball future. The 1919 scandal ended all of that.

THE 1919 BLACK SOX SCANDAL

While many had and continue to have sympathy for Joe Jackson, many also feel for Buck Weaver. There is no evidence that shows that Weaver did anything to contribute to the 1919 World Series defeat. His crime, according to the baseball powers-that-be, was his silence. Yet, many others did nothing even though there was something obviously going wrong in the 1919 World Series. And that included Charles Comiskey.

John "Shano" Collins led off the 1919 World Series with a single to center. A versatile player, Collins had his best year in 1920, when he hit .303. He had no knowledge of or role in the 1919 fix.

BASEBALL'S INFAMOUS YEAR

Two of the most notorious of the Black Sox, Swede Risberg and Chick Gandil are standing next to each other during the 1919 season. Joe Jackson described Risberg as "a hard guy." After the Series, owner Comiskey hired a private detective to check on any strange outlays of cash by any of the suspected cheaters. The only one showing anything was Gandil. Despite this, Comiskey offered Gandil a contract for the 1920 season. Gandil refused it, and left major-league baseball. The only one who truly profited from the 1919 Series was Gandil, even though he never admitted guilt.

Fred McMillin was an unlikely player to be part of the fix. But there are all kinds of ways to throw a baseball game. Any player, star or not, would have the capability to contribute to a loss.

Nemo Leibold had been contacted by friends and associates for inside info on the 1919 World Series and responded by not responding. He refused to be compromised. Despite going 1 for 18 in the Series, Leibold was never suspected of any wrongdoing.

The $1.10 bleacher admission is a pretty reasonable price for a World Series—even in 1919. Charles Comiskey was one owner who did what he could to keep ticket prices affordable, even though he was accused of being less than generous with his players.

Right in the middle of this 1917 photograph of White Sox outfielders is Oscar "Happy" Felsch. Felsch was a big RBI man for the team, but in the 1919 Series hit only .192 and picked up three RBIs, although it was said he was robbed of a couple of hits by the Reds defense. Felsch had his best year in 1920 when he drove in 115, but then came the 1921 trial and the end of his career.

BASEBALL'S INFAMOUS YEAR

3

TWO TRIALS

The main goal of the American legal system is to allow the accused to be judged by a jury of his or her peers. In a trial, evidence is presented and witnesses are heard. Finally, a verdict is rendered and there is supposed to be some kind of emotional closure, if not justice. Ideally, the guilty are held accountable for their actions, and the innocent are set free.

The two central court cases involving the Black Sox scandal accomplished little except for adding to the controversy, debate, and hard feelings connected to the 1919 World Series.

There were no specific laws concerning a professional baseball player throwing a game. If a shortstop wanted to let a ground ball scoot between his legs and hop into left field, he could do that without fear of going to prison. But because of the connection to gambling and the fact that people had paid to see a legitimate World Series, the eight White Sox players were charged with defrauding the public, along with conspiracy to commit a confidence game, conspiracy to injure the business of the American League, and finally, to injure the business of Charles A. Comiskey. Their trial took place in 1921.

The eight men were found not guilty, but not guilty of what? In his instructions to the jury, Judge Hugo Friend stated that jury members had to establish "intent" of fraud. The throwing of baseball games was almost secondary. Even the players understood that this legal tight-roping favored them. (Ironically, when Friend died of a heart attack in 1966, he was listening to a radio broadcast of a White Sox–Indians game.)

In the *Eight Men Out* movie, the Black Sox were shown drinking and celebrating into the night, assuming they had been cleared of wrongdoing and would be playing baseball again.

Kenesaw Mountain Landis thought otherwise.

Landis had been recently installed into the newly created office of Major League Baseball commissioner. Having the immense power of acting in the best interests of Major League Baseball as he saw it, Landis was not impressed with the jury verdict. (Strange, since he had been a federal judge himself, and still held that position at the time of his appointment as commissioner.) He informed the eight Black Sox that they would never play major league baseball again. And he never wavered from that edict.

American League president Ban Johnson backed Landis, saying, "The trial uncovered the greatest crime it was possible to commit in baseball. The fact they were freed does not alter the conditions one iota or minimize the magnitude of the offense."

So much for vindication, at least in the eyes of Major League Baseball.

In 1924, Joe Jackson sued the White Sox for breach of contract in a Milwaukee trial. He had signed a three-year deal in 1920 but the contract was terminated due to the Black Sox scandal.

Jackson's real argument was that he had played an honest 1919 World Series. Jackson needed 10 out of the 12 jurors to rule in his favor. He was elated when 11 of the 12 came out on his side, thinking his reputation had been restored.

Not necessarily so. Judge John Gregory vacated the verdict with a scolding of the jury and accused Jackson of perjury. Jackson was even jailed briefly.

Thomas Cannon, grandson of Joe Jackson's lawyer, would describe Gregory as an upright jurist, saying, "I think his sense of right and wrong was offended by Jackson's contrary testimony in the Chicago criminal and Milwaukee civil trials, both under oath."

Two trials. Two verdicts favoring the Black Sox. Yet, the 1921 trial was called a sham by many, and Gregory lectured the 1924 jury on their lack of wisdom. Instead of clarifying what had happened in 1919, the picture only became murkier. The 1919 Black Sox were not actually cleared of throwing games, and Jackson's reputation took a hit even when he temporarily won a legal battle. He would fight to restore his reputation for the remainder of his life. Debate over the whole scandal continued with no sense of closure, legally or emotionally.

In a way, the 1919 White Sox and owner Charles Comiskey are still on trial today. A real verdict is unclear. The baseball jury seems to be hung.

Eddie Collins poses with his son sometime after the scandal broke. After the team returned to Chicago following a late August 1920 three-game series in Boston in which they were swept, Collins visited Charles Comiskey and accused his teammates of throwing the Boston series just as they did the World Series the year before. If the second baseman was right, the corruption on the team was deeper and more pervasive than imagined.

Chicago Tribune sports reporter James Crusinberry made a list of 1919 Chicago White Sox players. Although it is not dated, it was compiled over 20 years after the scandal, because he lists Bill James as deceased and James died in 1942. Crusinberry had tried to write about the 1919 fix in July 1920. After a strange encounter arranged by Kid Gleason, Crusinberry got details of the fix by "listening" to conversation between Gleason and gambler Abe Attell. Attell even apologized to Gleason but said he had been desperate for money. But sports editor Harvey Woodruff refused to run the story for fear of legal action against the paper. There was also a general feeling of not wanting to believe the worst. Things began to break open a short time later.

THE 1919 BLACK SOX SCANDAL

49

If there is any confusion surrounding the 1919 scandal, much of it centers around Shoeless Joe Jackson (right.) He denied making any confession to a grand jury, and also denied admitting guilt to a disillusioned boy after coming out of a grand jury hearing. He finally denied that any meeting with a boy happened at all. For the remainder of his life, he pointed to his .375 Series average as proof of his honest play, although skeptics said he did most of his hitting once the Series was out of hand. And those same skeptics also scoff at the idea that the naïve Jackson didn't understand what was happening in 1919 because of his illiteracy. One thing has never been debated; Joe Jackson was one of the best hitters of his time, maybe of all time.

It is difficult to identify anyone in this crowd except for Kenesaw Mountain Landis. Landis, seated alone in the rear at left, can easily be spotted with his snow-white hair and ever-present, self-righteous scowl. He is credited for saving major-league baseball with his resoluteness toward the Black Sox. He probably had no choice, considering the crisis baseball faced. However, the baseball establishment never truly investigated just what really happened in 1919.

Buck Weaver and Fred McMullin pose with attorney Thomas Nash. Nash, in questioning witnesses Kid Gleason and Ray Schalk, asked if they thought the accused players had performed to the best of their ability. This seemed odd, since both Gleason and Schalk were pushed to the edge of violence because of their suspicions. Even more odd, the prosecution objected to the line of questioning on both occasions. Both times, their objections were upheld and neither Gleason nor Schalk were allowed to express their opinion. McMullin is an odd character in the scandal. He was not a starting player during the regular season, getting only 170 at-bats. In the Series, he had two plate appearances with a hit, so his influence on the outcome was practically nonexistent. Yet it was said he pocketed $5,000 of gamblers' money. He was banned with the rest.

White Sox players sit on a different kind of bench during their trial. Instead of a manager, they have their attorney. Although they were found not guilty, the 1919 scandal convicted and sentenced them in a different way. Buck Weaver, as usual, has the biggest smile. Perhaps he thought he would be completely exonerated. Kenesaw Landis didn't see it that way.

THE 1919 BLACK SOX SCANDAL

51

This 1922 team photograph was described as "No Stars Left." In reality, considering the decimation of the White Sox roster, the 1922 squad did okay by itself by finishing with an even 77-77 mark. But the team would not finish higher than fifth for the next 11 years. Obviously, the scandal had a long-lasting effect, and it is sad to think of what could have been.

```
C. H. 64045 "S" (SLUG) GANDIL.

    GANDIL SAYS ALL WHITE SOX INVOLVED IN
                   PAY OFF.

Chicago, Jan. 3-27:- According to a copy-
righted story in the ElPaso Times this morning,
Chick Gandil, now manager of the Chino baseball
team at Hurley, New Mexico, admitted that he
collected the money and made the arrangements
wherein the White Sox bought a series from the
Detroit Tigers in 1917, and further added that
every member of the White Sox were involved.

Photo is of Chick Gandil.
```

This journalistic "slug" tells a damning story told by Chick Gandil regarding an alleged payoff by White Sox players to the Detroit Tigers for losing two consecutive doubleheaders toward the end of the 1917 pennant race. The reputation of the White Sox continued to suffer even with Commissioner Landis clearing all players of these accusations. Landis declared those four games legitimate.

Pitcher Bill James did some limited duty on the 1919 White Sox and was not implicated in the fix. However, he played with the 1917 Tigers and appeared in both games in the September 3 doubleheader. In game one, he did well enough pitching two innings, giving up one run and two hits. In game two, he was tagged for five runs in three innings, although three of those runs were unearned. James took the loss in a 14-8 defeat. He went 3-1 for the rest of the last month of the season and finished with a career-best ERA of 2.09. If James "sloughed off" when facing the White Sox, it has not been fully proved.

THE 1919 BLACK SOX SCANDAL

> — 67077 "P AND A PHOTOS." CHICAGO.
> OTO SHOWS Bill James, former Detroit
> cher)
>
> ED AS PAYOFF MAN IN "SCANDAL OF 1917"
>
> l James, former Detroit pitcher, has
> n named by Chick Gandil, banished White
> first baseman, as the player to whom he
> ndil) turned over a pot of money to be
> ned over to certain members of the Detroit
> b for "throwing" four games in September
> 7.   James will face Gandil before
> ge Landis in Chicago, who is supervising
> hearing of the latest sensational flareup
> organized baseball.

Did the Detroit Tigers actually throw any games to the White Sox in 1917? Would any money truly be worth it? How common a practice was this? Regardless, Major League Baseball did not need its eyes blackened any further.

> Shortstop
> baseman A
> implicated men in the baseball scandal now
> on trial in Chicago. Risberg is supposed to
> have received $5,000 and Gandil $50,000.
> Gandil is supposed to have been the prime
> mover in the affair. He was not with the
> team this season.
> Copyright Keystone View Co. —sss

This description nails Chick Gandil. Moneywise, he came out the best of all the Black Sox. While most talk about the greatness of Joe Jackson, Chick Gandil was considered one of the better first baseman of his day. That position is often underrated, but a good first baseman can help teams get out of many innings. Gandil was another example of talent gone to waste.

Would anybody like to meet this guy in a dark alley? If anyone made out on the 1919 scandal, it was Chick Gandil. Charles Comiskey hired a private detective to check on the suspected 1919 cheaters to see if any of them had any strange outlays of cash. The only one who seemed to have come into any real money was Gandil. Despite this, Comiskey offered him a contract for the 1920 season, but Gandil refused it and walked away from major-league baseball. However, he never fully walked away from the scandal.

In this 1929 image, Comiskey Park has a capacity crowd, and it looks like winning has returned to the South Side. However, the team barely avoided ending up in last place, losing 93 and finishing just two games ahead of cellar-dwelling Boston. The Chicago team that had a successful season that year was the Cubs, who went to the World Series. The North Siders lost the Series in five to the Philadelphia Athletics. In game four, the Athletics wiped out an 8-0 lead with a 10-run seventh.

THE 1919 BLACK SOX SCANDAL

The first All-Star Game was played at Comiskey Park on July 6, 1933. In this photograph, Lou Gehrig is labeled No. 3 and Babe Ruth is No. 4. Ruth hit a third-inning two-run homer into the upper deck in right to provide the difference in a 4-2 American League win. Jimmy Dykes represented the White Sox and got two hits. Tony Cuccinello, who was a White Sox coach in the 1950s and 1960s, had one plate appearance for the National League.

The National League All-Star squad was managed by John McGraw, whose New York Giants had faced the White Sox in the 1917 World Series. Frankie Frisch homered for the National League. Frisch was elected to the Hall of Fame in 1947.

The brain trust of the White Sox during the late 1920s consisted of Harry Grabiner, who held a position that would be similar to today's general manager, and J. Louis Comiskey, son of the owner. The men are standing on the back end of a touring train the team used to connect with fans. Grabiner handled many of the day-to-day operations of the club after Charles Comiskey turned reclusive in the aftermath of the scandal. J. Louis Comiskey was viewed as a decent man, but he fought chronic illnesses and died only a few years after his father. Grabiner worked for the club for 30 years.

Charles Comiskey, visibly aged, talks with his only son, J. Louis. The younger Comiskey was considered to be a gentle, likable man. This meeting took place just months before Charles died. J. Louis would live for only a few more years, passing away at age 54.

This happy photograph shows J. Louis Comiskey with his five-year-old son Chuck. Chuck remained tied to the White Sox until he sold his interests to Arthur Allyn in 1962. He attended the last game in the park that bore his family name on September 30, 1990.

58 TWO TRIALS

4

RECOVERY

During the 1950s, Americans experienced a new fear. The country's archrival, the Soviet Union, had a mentally unbalanced leader and a nuclear arsenal. A war with the Soviets would be more than just a military confrontation; it could mean complete annihilation and perhaps the end of the world as people knew it. The nation felt as if it lived under an atomic mushroom cloud.

That is one reason why some Chicagoans panicked at 10:30 pm on September 22, 1959. For five minutes, the city's air raid sirens blared, and it was thought Soviet missiles were heading toward the United States. Many headed to shelters or low ground, but could they truly hide?

Was the United States really under a nuclear attack? No, the Chicago White Sox had just won the American League pennant.

In 1959, the American League was an eight-team, one-division league. A first-place finish was an immediate ticket to the World Series. On that noisy night, the White Sox played their closest pursuer, the Cleveland Indians, in Cleveland. Some 54,293 hoped the Indians could stave off elimination. For a moment, it looked like they would.

The White Sox led 4-2 in the bottom of the ninth with reliever Gerry Staley on the mound. But Cleveland had loaded the bases with one out. Indians second baseman Vic Power rapped a grounder toward short. Luis Aparicio fielded the ball near second, stepped on the bag, and threw to first baseman Ted Kluszewski to complete the double play and secure the win for the Sox.

In Chicago, the celebration began with the sirens.

Robert Quinn, Chicago fire commissioner, set off the sirens in keeping with a Chicago City Council resolution that read, "Be it further resolved that bells ring, whistles blow, bands play, and general joy be unconfined when the coveted pennant has been won by the heroes of 35th Street."

Despite the panic, the blasting sirens were appropriate. For the 40 years since the Black Sox scandal, the White Sox franchise had been quiet. After 1920, the team never came all that close to winning a pennant. Finally, in 1959, they won, and they won in ways that would have made the 1919 team proud.

Their leading home run hitter was catcher Sherm Lollar, who had 22. No one had over 100 RBIs. They won with speed, defense, and pitching. Second baseman Nellie Fox, who won the American League MVP Award, was a singles hitter and a great bunter. Fox had 717 plate appearances and struck out only 13 times. Luis Aparicio led the league with 56 stolen bases. Center fielder Jim Landis tied with two other players by getting 13 bunt hits. Aging pitcher Early Wynn won 22 and captured the Cy Young Award. Their manager, Al Lopez, was the only non-Yankee manager to win an American League pennant during the 1950s. (He won one other in 1954 with Cleveland.)

The White Sox won the first game of the World Series against the Los Angeles Dodgers 11-0 in Comiskey Park. But they lost four out of the next five. No World Series noise would come until 2005.

The White Sox endured other disappointments during the 1960s as the American League pennant continued to elude them. But the team had a string of winning seasons from 1951 to 1967 that included seven 90-plus-wins years, the 1959 pennant, and five second-place finishes. In 1964, the Sox barely missed a pennant when they picked up 98 victories and won their last nine. They finished one game behind—who else—the Yankees.

The 1967 team, like its 1917 counterpart, was lost in history. Despite hitting only 89 homers as a club and having no starting players with a batting average over .241, the 1967 White Sox stayed in a four-team pennant race until the last days of the season. Finally, they were exposed for the weak offensive team they were and were eliminated with three games left in the season. Yet, like the 1917 team, no one seems to remember them.

During these 17 seasons, Sox fans were frustrated because their club could not get past a Yankee team filled with Hall of Fame candidates. But winning and respectability had finally returned to a franchise haunted by scandal. The White Sox were never again accused of selling out 1919 style.

Frank Lane was the White Sox general manager from 1948 to 1955 and was largely responsible for one of the most successful decades in team history. Lane acquired players like Minnie Minoso, Nelson Fox, Sherm Lollar, and Billy Pierce. With the success that began in 1951, the team finally stepped back from the carnage of the Black Sox scandal.

A young Nelson Fox is covering second base. Fox couldn't hit home runs, so he made no effort to do so. Instead, he did what is expected of a good middle infielder: get on base and play good defense. With Luis Aparicio, Fox formed the best double-play combination in team history. In 1959, Fox won the MVP Award, although there had been some talk of making Fox and Aparicio co-MVPs, which wasn't a bad idea. A team can't win unless there is strength up the middle. Fox anchored that middle for the Sox for 14 seasons.

Simply said, Luis Aparicio was the greatest shortstop to wear a White Sox uniform and was one of the greatest of all time at that position. He was a smart player. As he aged, Aparicio lost some of his range. So, he studied American League hitters in order to position himself in a strategic manner. When he heard the White Sox were going to trade him, he said it was vital that he stay in the American League because he knew nothing about National League hitters. The Sox obliged him by sending him to Boston. Luis Aparicio, the player who helped define the Go-Go White Sox of the 1950s, was elected to the Hall of Fame in 1984.

When was the last time readers saw white wall tires like this? Notice the small structures in front of Comiskey Park. Fans would buy tickets at any of these buildings depending on where they wanted to sit. Buying tickets online really isn't all that different. It is just a matter of technology.

The fleet-footed Jim Landis added to the strong up-the-middle defense of the 1959 White Sox. In game one of the 1959 World Series, Landis picked up three hits and scored three times.

Sherm Lollar was sometimes criticized for not showing intensity on the field. Yet he was a strong force behind the plate for 12 seasons with the White Sox. He had his best overall offensive year in 1959, and his team needed it. One could only steal so many bases. Lollar was strong defensively, winning three Gold Gloves in his career.

RECOVERY

Partly because of injuries, Dick Donovan didn't have his best year in 1959 as he went 9-10. But he did win a key game late in the season against the Indians. He outlasted Cleveland's Jim Perry, winning 2-0 with a complete game five-hitter.

Al Smith is shown here in a happier picture. In the fifth inning of game two of the 1959 Series, Smith went back to the wall trying to snare a drive hit by Dodger Charlie Neal. The attempt was futile, as Neal's shot sailed into the seats for a home run. A fan, wanting a souvenir, knocked his beer off the top of the wall. The liquid, looking like a small, silver waterfall, splashed down on Smith. "It was in my nose and everywhere," Smith said. For Smith and Sox fans, it was the most disappointing moment of 1959.

Larry Doby made history by being the first African American to play in the American League in 1947. He managed the 1978 White Sox during the second half of the season. He was almost set up to fail with an undermanned club that didn't finish near .500. In the year this photograph was taken, 1956, Doby hit 24 homers and knocked in 102. He was elected to the Hall of Fame in 1998.

The excitement of the World Series coming to Chicago is illustrated by the jumbled activity right outside Comiskey Park. Police are directing traffic as a two-toned car makes its way through the intersection. At first, the author thought the car was the failed Edsel. After further research, it was discovered that the Edsel was much uglier than this. The car does have the rear fins that were characteristic of the 1950s.

Al Lopez was one of the greatest of all White Sox managers, winning 840 while losing 650. The 97-year-old Lopez anxiously watched his White Sox play in the 2005 World Series. Glad to see his team finally win a championship, Lopez died four days later a happy man.

Bill Veeck was easily the most flamboyant man to run the White Sox. He was a master showman and carefully honed his image for the media. The team finally went to the World Series after a 40-year absence under his leadership. He sold the team in 1961. Veeck returned to repurchase the White Sox in late 1975, preventing a transfer of the franchise to Seattle. Veeck had his critics. He was faulted for trades made after the 1959 Series, and many weren't crazy about some of his promotions. However, his influence on Chicago baseball should not be underestimated.

Early Wynn, at least from his grip, looks like he is throwing a knuckleball. Wynn won 22 in the pennant-winning year of 1959, and pitched seven scoreless innings in an 11-0 first game of the World Series. Wynn, a good-hitting pitcher who hit 17 home runs in his career, was in the final stages of his time as a pitcher in this game. He was hanging on so he could win 300 games. He picked up that 300th win in 1963 when he pitched for Cleveland. It was the last win of his career.

Bob Shaw is warming up for his start in the second game of the 1959 World Series against the Dodgers. Shaw and the White Sox lost the game 4-3 when a tying run was cut down at the plate in the bottom of the eighth. Shaw had a career year in 1959, winning 18 and posting an ERA of 2.69.

THE 1919 BLACK SOX SCANDAL 69

Left-hander Billy Pierce spent the entire 1950s with the White Sox. Except for 1954, he had double-digit wins every year and two 20-win seasons. Pierce would long be identified with the White Sox. In 1970, he spent a season as a TV color analyst and tried to sound upbeat during a 106-loss season. His statue sits on the outfield concourse of Guaranteed Rate Field.

Jim Rivera, known as "Jungle Jim," was a fixture on the White Sox during the 1950s. A colorful guy, Rivera said to John Kennedy after getting a presidential autograph in 1961, "What's this? This is just scribble. I can hardly make it out. You'll have to do better than this, John."

Minnie Minoso, one of the most memorable of White Sox players, played in five different decades: from 1949 to 1964, and then eight at-bats as a DH in 1976 and two plate appearances in 1980. More importantly, Minoso was one of the best all-around players the White Sox ever had. His number was retired in 1983.

The talented Juan Pizzaro won 131 games, but baseball observers thought he had real potential and should have won more. He played for eight different teams. Known for his late-night carousing, Pizzaro had his best year in 1964, when he won 19 while with the Sox.

Gary Peters was one of the best left-handed pitchers in the majors during the 1960s. In the 1967 All-Star game, Peters struck out Willie Mays, Roberto Clemente, Orlando Cepeda, and Dick Allen and pitched three perfect innings. On September 13 of that year, Peters went 11 innings against the Indians and gave up one hit. The White Sox won the game 1-0 in 17 innings. An excellent hitter, Peters was used as a pinch hitter, and on a couple of occasions hit higher than ninth.

Tommy John was part of the great 1967 pitching staff that threw 24 shutouts. John eventually went through what was to become known as "Tommy John surgery." His left pitching arm was repaired with a tendon from his right wrist. After the surgery, John picked up three 20-win seasons and finished with 288 wins in a 26-year career.

Right-handed pitcher Joe Horlen is leading off third base six years before the installation of the DH. Horlen, a hard-luck pitcher who had an excellent ERA but relatively few wins, finally had a breakthrough season in 1967 when he won 19. Horlen threw a no-hitter on September 10 against the hard-hitting Detroit Tigers to reverse the momentum of a crushing loss the day before, when Detroit wiped out a 3-0 Sox lead with a seven-run ninth. During his no-hitter, Horlen was hit by a pitch on the inside of his knee and could not sit when his team was hitting. He paced the dugout before returning to the mound.

It was said Ted Kluszewski's biceps were so large he couldn't wear normal shirts. Here, he stands in the on-deck circle in a sleeveless jersey. He smacked two home runs in game one of the 1959 Series. After the game, a teenage boy visited him in the locker room with one of the home run souvenirs. With a huge smile, Kluszewski autographed the ball. Then he went home to have a quiet dinner with his wife, not thinking much of what he did.

THE 1919 BLACK SOX SCANDAL

Everyone is at attention during the national anthem right before game one of the 1959 World Series. The "Chesterfield" scoreboard would be replaced by the fireworks-shooting "Monster" in 1960. For almost 60 years now, White Sox home runs have been celebrated with fireworks.

74   RECOVERY

The weak-hitting White Sox needed an RBI man during the early 1960s and thought they found one in third baseman Pete Ward. Ward knocked in 84 in 1963 and followed that with 94 the next year. But he suffered a back injury in an automobile accident in April 1965. He showed occasional spurts of power, but was never the same hitter. The White Sox would have two other third basemen with serious back injuries: Bill Melton and Joe Crede.

Feisty Don Buford played second and third base for the White Sox from 1963 to 1967. His biggest hit for the team came in the middle of a four-team pennant race on September 14, 1967. The White Sox were in a scoreless tie with Cleveland in the bottom of the tenth. With two out, Buford hit a walk-off grand slam. The win helped the White Sox stay within 2 ½ games of first-place Boston, although they were still in fourth place. Buford was then traded to Baltimore, where he played on three World Series teams.

THE 1919 BLACK SOX SCANDAL

Ken Berry played center field with abandon. On one occasion, he tried to run down a fly ball by throwing his whole body in a backwards flip over the short center-field fence in a 1968 game at Comiskey. Unfortunately, he couldn't snare the drive, which turned out to be a home run hit by Tony Oliva of the Twins. Berry won Gold Gloves in 1970 and 1972.

Tommy McCraw was a fixture at first base for the White Sox during the 1960s. On September 29, 1967, a loss eliminated the Sox from the pennant race. McCraw had a rough first inning during the game against the Washington Senators. First, he made an error. Then, with one out and two on, Senator Fred Valentine hit a pop foul to the first-base side. Normally, McCraw would have made the catch, but a camera well had been installed behind first in anticipation of a World Series. The foul fly fell out of McCraw's reach and into the well. Valentine, given new life, singled to left and drove in what turned out to be the only run of the game. The White Sox, getting four little hits off a pitcher who had not won game in six weeks, lost 1-0, and their pennant dreams ended.

Knuckleball pitcher Hoyt Wilhelm spent six of his 21 years in the major leagues with the White Sox. In five of those six seasons, his ERA was under two. Most of his career was spent in the bullpen, and he appeared in 1,070 games.

During a mound conference, manager Eddie Stanky looks up at lefty Gary Peters during the pennant-contending year of 1967. Although the White Sox were in first place for a good part of the season, the weak-hitting team was accused of being "boring." In a tirade to the media, Stanky defended his team, saying, "We're last in homers, we're last in hitting and we're last in war and peace. But we're first in guts and determination." When the White Sox were eliminated after the 1-0 loss against the Senators, an emotionally shaken Stanky left a postgame press conference in tears.

John Allyn bought controlling interests of the White Sox from his brother Art in September 1969. The images he is looking at here depict a White Sox resurgence of sorts in the early 1970s. However, Allyn didn't have the financial resources to maintain a major-league team in the long run. On one occasion, the club ordered six dozen bats but only three dozen were delivered. Allyn explained it to catcher Ed Herrmann: "We're a little short." In late 1975, Allyn sold the team to a group headed by Bill Veeck—saving the team from being moved to Seattle.

Arthur Allyn, White Sox owner during most of the 1960s, is testing the new Astroturf installed in the Comiskey Park infield in time for the 1969 season. The turf was meant to help weak White Sox hitters sneak ground balls into the outfield for much-needed base hits. There was no evidence that it helped the Sox offense. The turf was ripped out in 1976.

THE 1919 BLACK SOX SCANDAL

Comiskey Park had a little bit of technology. Home plate umpires could renew their supply of baseballs from an underground basket. Opponents accused the White Sox of storing baseballs in a refrigerator as a way to help their excellent pitching. Try to hit a cold baseball and see how far it goes. The White Sox vehemently denied these scandalous accusations.

5

DREAMS

At first, it seemed like a strange premise. Not an Iowa farmer being compelled to plow a cornfield over and turn it into a baseball field. Not that he fantasized about an old-time deceased player walking out of the corn stalks to take his place on the newly contoured field. And not even that the farmer actually spoke to the player and that the player was then joined by others wearing the same old-time uniforms.

No, what was strange was that these fantasy players were not from a historic championship team or even a collection of Hall-of-Fame all-stars, but rather the 1919 White Sox. This baseball fantasy centered around a disgraced team that threw a World Series and nearly destroyed the American game of baseball.

History had already passed judgement on eight White Sox players, who became known as the Black Sox. They betrayed their team's owner, their teammates, and the game that was supposed to mean something to them. Their punishment consisted of a lifetime ban from playing. No protests of innocence or acts of contrition would ever be considered. They could not be allowed on any baseball field anywhere or fans would never believe that major-league baseball was the real thing. All appeals to allow them to play again were ignored by the commissioner.

The movie, of course, is *Field of Dreams*, which stars Kevin Costner and James Earl Jones. In the tear-jerking ending, the 1919 White Sox are allowed to play baseball again and the Costner and Jones characters experience a redemption of their own. The bitterness for these characters and the 1919 Black Sox seems to vanish in the cornfield.

But this is just a movie, right? The premise is just a fantasy, right?

Betty Boeckenstedt is a member of the Lansing family that owns the farm that was used in the making of *Field of Dreams*. Boeckenstedt recalled a morning shortly after the movie had been released. The baseball field was still there in the midst of the farm. The bleachers on the first-base line remained. Her brother was having breakfast before going to work and looked out to see a lone figure sitting in the bleachers. The man was from New York and said something pushed him to drive out to see the movie site. He handed over a Yankees cap as a token of appreciation.

But *Field of Dreams* is just a movie, right? The premise is just a fantasy, right?

The movie site is now open to the public and attracts 115,000 visitors a year. According to operations manager Roman Weinberg (oddly, Weinberg is a Cubs fan with a "W" towel hanging by his desk), the movie site has visitors from all over the world. He says that many like to take the field and play a game, including one day a group of nuns in their habits.

Weinberg encouraged the author to take a walk on the neatly manicured field. The pitcher's mound sprouts up in the middle of the infield looking like a dab of butter melting into the grids of a waffle. Anyone who has played one inning of baseball will say that one fantasy is to hit a game winning home run. But here a person will look out into the corn field and wait. Wait for players to appear wearing old fashioned uniforms to take their positions. Only the players will not be labeled as the 1919 Black Sox. They will represent the 1919 Chicago White Sox, American League champions. And now those White Sox are finally going to gain the long-sought redemption by playing baseball like it was meant to be played, like they could have done 100 years ago.

But *Field of Dreams* is just a movie, right? The premise is just a fantasy, right?

Tell that to the 115,000 or so who visit the site every year. Tell that to people who saw *Field of Dreams* and wept as they watched the last scene.

The Field of Dreams Movie Site is marked by this colorful sign. The baseball field can be seen at left, and the white farmhouse is at the back of the lot. An extensive search was done for a proper site for the movie, and some farmers were not interested in participating in the project. (Courtesy of the Field of Dreams Movie Site.)

This simple structure operates as a souvenir shop at the front entrance of the movie site. The farmhouse is directly behind. The word "If" can be seen on the white picket fence, part of the phrase, "If you build it, they will come." One of the souvenirs sold is a T-shirt with a graphic of a boy and his father playing catch. The graphic emulates the ending and emotional scene of the Kevin Costner character getting a second chance of making peace with his father by playing a simple but powerful game of catch. (Courtesy of the Field of Dreams Movie site.)

This home looks like it could sit on any farm, or any residential block for that matter. Now it is part of American movie history. The main floor had to be renovated to give it an early American look. The stove used in the film remained, as movers convinced the Lansing family to keep it because it would be hard to move. And, of course, the Field of Dreams sign cannot be missed. (Courtesy of the Field of Dreams Movie Site.)

The Field of Dreams is the place where Joe Jackson and the 1919 White Sox got a second chance. A variety of events occur at the field, including weddings and an ex–major leaguers All-Star game. In one of these, Frank Thomas hit an arching home run deep into the corn. (Courtesy of the Field of Dreams Movie Site.)

The kitchen is shown here as it appears in the *Field of Dreams* movie. The filmmakers wanted to ensure that the décor had a realistic image of a Midwestern American home. (Courtesy of the Field of Dreams Movie Site.)

Standing below the street sign honoring Shoeless Joe Jackson are Roman Weinberg and Clarence Heacock of the Field of Dreams Movie Site. The window by Weinberg's desk looks out onto the baseball field on the Lansing Farm. He told the author he looks out the window anytime he needs to cheer himself up. Heacock, outfitted in a 1919 White Sox uniform, is a tour guide at the site. He can tell you anything about the *Field of Dreams* movie and how it was made. When Heacock provides a tour of the home, two movies are playing on separate TVs. One, of course, is *Field of Dreams*. The other is *Harvey*, a 1950 release starring Jimmy Stewart. The Stewart character speaks to a six-and-a-half-foot rabbit named Harvey that only he sees—just as the Costner character, for a time, is the only one to see and speak with Shoeless Joe Jackson. (Courtesy of the Field of Dreams Movie Site)

Eddie Stanky, a throwback type of baseball man, stands at the edge of the White Sox dugout in 1967. Pitcher Joe Horlen said that when he wasn't pitching, he would sit next to Stanky on the bench. Stanky would analyze the game and even ask for Horlen's opinion. This provides an image of a father teaching his son about baseball. About a year after Stanky died in 1999, Horlen said to the author: "Eddie Stanky was the only manager who ever fined me, and I still loved him."

A fireworks show has just ended after a 5-4 White Sox win over the Minnesota Twins on May 17, 1967. The giant, square light towers brightly illuminated the vast Comiskey Park outfield. Comiskey Park was a beautiful sight at night, and rather similar to a field of dreams.

This image is aptly titled *Afternoon in Center Field*. Now, telephone wires extend over the middle of the field. It was thought that the field would lose some of its charm if the wires could be seen, so $80,000 was spent in moving them for the movie. The players came out of the corn rows in right field. (Courtesy of the Field of Dreams Movie Site.)

6

OVERACHIEVING

The early fall night of September 26, 1989, was cold and lonely at old Comiskey. A little less than 7,000 braved the wintry conditions to watch a relatively meaningless game against the Minnesota Twins. The White Sox sat in the cellar of the Western Division with no realistic chance of finishing higher. The Twins, World Series winners just two years earlier, were not contending for the postseason and were hoping to finish with a .500 season. They wouldn't make it. Needless to say, suspense was not part of the game.

To add to the pain suffered by White Sox fans, an image from another game flashed on the scoreboard jumbotron. The Chicago Cubs had beaten the Montreal Expos (now the Washington Nationals) 3-2. More importantly, the Cubs had clinched the Eastern Division. As Cubs players danced around in Montreal, their fans hoped the team was on its way to its first World Series since 1945. For the White Sox, it had now been 70 years since the Black Sox scandal and the South Siders had only been to one World Series. In one seven-game stretch during the early part of the 1989 season, the Sox were outscored 63-14. Needless to say, they lost all seven.

Meanwhile, the White Sox lost in the Comiskey Park tundra 7-1, managing a meager three hits. A young Sammy Sosa, acquired in a trade with the Texas Rangers, was in the Sox lineup and went 0 for 3 with two strikeouts. Four games remained on the schedule. If it wasn't for the Cubs going to the playoffs, White Sox fans would have looked forward to the season ending.

As to the expectations for 1990, the last year of old Comiskey Park? There weren't any. The White Sox had just suffered their fourth consecutive losing season and fifth of the last six.

Then a strange thing occurred. The White Sox began winning.

By June 14, the Sox were 36-20, two games behind first place and defending world champion Oakland. The A's came to Chicago for a four-game series and won three. The champs had asserted themselves, and were not a bit concerned about a challenge from the puny White Sox.

But then the Sox traveled to Oakland the next weekend for a three-game series. Chicago swept the series, winning the final game on a home run by Dan Pasqua in the 10th inning. Pasqua had connected off of starter Dave Stewart.

Stewart had 20-win seasons in the three previous years and would get one more in 1990. He had such a mean disposition he could break a person's face just by looking at him. Stewart had no respect for the White Sox, even in defeat.

"They seem to think that they had some pretty good ballplayers," Stewart said. "There aren't many players over there who could hold my jock as far as I'm concerned."

Jeff Torborg, Sox manager in 1990, told the author in late 2018, "Stewart was right. We couldn't hold his jock. Not that we wanted to."

The White Sox did have closer Bobby Thigpen, who set a then season record of 57 saves. But they did not have a 20-game winner, or any hitter with more than 20 home runs or 100 RBIs. The team boasted one .300 hitter—Frank Thomas—but the young Thomas hadn't been called up until August 2. Shortstop Ozzie Guillen referred to the 1990 team as "smurfs." Otherwise, the 1990 squad did the little things well. They advanced runners, turned the double play, and played sound and fundamental baseball. In other words, they played in similar ways to the 1919 team that should have won that year's World Series. The 1990 Sox even won a game 4-0 when they got no-hit.

Yet the 1990 White Sox won 94 games, good for third-best in major-league baseball. They had the bad luck of playing in the same division as Oakland, which won 103. Speaking of Oakland, what did Dave Stewart say about the Sox after Chicago beat Oakland two out of three in mid-September?

"That ball club has a lot to be proud of," Stewart said. "They got a lot to hold their heads up about."

The last game at Comiskey was played on September 30 against the Seattle Mariners. The White Sox won in typical 1990 style, 2-1, with the help of a bad-hop triple. Bobby Thigpen picked up his last save of the season.

Many of the 42,849 stayed for some time after the last out was recorded and held up signs like "Good-Bye Old Friend," "Thanks for the Memories," and finally, "Years From Now, We'll Say, We Wuz Here." Attendance had increased by almost one million over 1989, and topped the two million mark for the first time since 1984.

The author told manager Torborg that the 1990 squad was one of the most-loved White Sox teams. Torborg said that television play-by-play man Ken Harrelson told him the same thing. The reason for this love was simple: the 1990 Chicago White Sox won games they should have lost. That beats losing World Series games they should have been won.

Without a doubt, Frank Thomas was the greatest hitter in Chicago White Sox history, rivaled only by Shoeless Joe Jackson. Thomas hit for power, for average, and to all fields with devastating authority. Possessing a great batting eye, Thomas drew 100 or more walks in a season 10 times in his career and rarely swung at a bad pitch. Injuries kept him from being a major factor in 2005 and also kept him from putting up even bigger career numbers. Thomas was elected to the Hall of Fame in 2014 and will always be known as "The Big Hurt." (Ron Vesely/Chicago White Sox.)

Ozzie Guillen, during his later playing days, is wearing a 1917 World Series uniform. Guillen played on the 94-game-winning 1990 team, and according to that team's manager, Jeff Torborg, had a big influence. Guillen was tabbed as one the team's captains (along with Carlton Fisk) and was viewed as a guiding veteran presence. The 1990 season also had a strong influence on Guillen as a manager. The scratching out of runs and winning close games became one of the trademarks of the 2005 world champion team Guillen managed. Although the 2005 club hit 200 home runs, it emulated the 1990 club by playing "small ball." (Ron Vesely/Chicago White Sox.)

Manager Jeff Torborg faces a media crunch during the surprise 1990 season. Toborg felt there was a strong emotional bond between the fans and the overachieving team. The final home game of 1990 was a tearful experience for both the team and the fans.

TV color analyst Tom Paciorek emcees ceremonies honoring catcher Carlton Fisk. The two were teammates on the 1983 "Winnin' Ugly" squad, the first White Sox team to win a division title. The prediction of a Hall of Fame induction for Fisk came true 10 years later, although he entered as a Boston Red Sox. Fisk hit one of the most memorable home runs in baseball history in the sixth game of the 1975 World Series against the Reds. His 12th-inning homer knocked off the left field foul pole, and Boston won 7-6.

This image shows team and fans standing during the national anthem during the final weekend at Comiskey Park. Around 120,000 attended the last three games, played against the Seattle Mariners. Seattle's Harold Reynolds made the last out when he grounded out to second baseman Scott Fletcher. Comiskey Park will always be remembered for its stately windows and "Monster" scoreboard. Unfortunately, it will also be remembered for its seats behind steel girders.

OVERACHIEVING

After the final game at Comiskey Park on September 30, 1990, a young Sammy Sosa waves to the over 42,000 in attendance. Jeff Torborg, team manager, told the author that the overachieving 1990 team truly bonded with their fans because of their sound fundamental play. Torborg said he saw fans holding hands with tears on their faces. The sentiment was real. During the season, fans often held up signs reading, "Doing the little things." There was a strong appreciation for a team that concentrated on executing fundamental plays. The emotions were bittersweet that year as many mourned the loss of the old ballpark. (Ron Vesely/Chicago White Sox.)

Banners like these hung over the outfield walls during many a season at Comiskey Park. Although fans knew the old park's time had come, it was hard for them to let go of the memories the stadium held. They were deeply saddened they would not be able to sit in the stadium again, and some even sat in the remains of the stadium at night after demolition took place during the day. These fans are saying good-bye after Comiskey's last game.

For a time, the two Comiskey Parks stood next to each other. The older park, as large as it was, seemed to be dwarfed by the new facility. Just under three million came to the new park in 1991, a season attendance record that lasted until 2006, the year after the world championship season. Some fans were terrified of the new park's high and steep upper deck. Eventually, the upper deck was remodeled and some of the higher rows were taken out.

The new Comiskey Park opened on April 18, 1991. It was the first new baseball stadium to open in Chicago in 76 years. Some 42,191 watched the White Sox get pummeled by the Detroit Tigers 16-0. Jack McDowell, the Sox pitching ace, started but did not make it out of the third inning. Years later, he told the author that some of the team thought they had angered the "gods of old Comiskey." An old uniform was burned behind second base as a sacrifice.

7

OVERCOMING HISTORY

The first-place White Sox heard haunting footsteps in August 2005. These footsteps were loud, heavy, and had the potential to invade the team's psyche. Once more, the White Sox could end up on the wrong side of history.

The team occupied first place from day one when they beat the Indians in typical 2005-style, 1-0. By the start of August, their lead over second-place Cleveland was a whopping 15 games. But over a long baseball season, every team—even good teams—have slumps. And, as the White Sox slumped in the heat of August with a seven-game losing streak, the pursuing Indians went on a hot streak. By August 22, the lead was down to eight.

A different history from 1919 dogged the White Sox. Chicago baseball teams had been to a collective two World Series during the entire post–World War II era. In those 60 years, both teams squandered the few championship chances they had in mind-numbing ways. Why should 2005 be any different?

Chicago Tribune columnist and Cub fan Eric Zorn truly hoped history was forecasting a White Sox failure that in some ways would shame the team worse than the 1919 Black Sox. He gloated in anticipation and baited the Sox faithful in an August 22 column that mentioned a "White Sox Toxic Number" (as opposed to a magic number):

"It's awfully fun watching you [White Sox fans] sweat and wring your hands and simply imagine how savory it will be if the Sox perpetrate a late-season collapse to make history forget all about the 1969 Cubs."

No Cubs fan of a certain generation will forget 1969, but Zorn's message was powerfully driven home. Think choke.

A few weeks later, *Tribune* cohort Phil Rogers wrote a story about several late-season flops in baseball history and speculated whether the White Sox would join a list of teams known for blowing big-time opportunities for fame and championships. Sox center fielder Aaron Rowand told the author almost 10 years later that the recounting of history and the speculation about a fold didn't affect the White Sox one bit. However, in 2005, Rowand confronted Rogers and voiced his displeasure, saying the story "sucked." And manager Ozzie Guillen admitted throwing up after losses and felt stung by fan boos. A *Tribune* photo symbolically showed Paul Konerko slipping down to one knee after popping up to end a September 19 loss to the Indians.

Exactly one month after his "toxic number" column, Eric Zorn must have been happy. The White Sox lost an 11-inning game to the Twins 4-1, and their lead was now a skimpy 1½ games. To Guillen, it seemed like the Indians won every day and their winning was not going to stop. And the White Sox had to finish their season with a three-game series in Cleveland.

Then history seemed to reverse itself.

On September 25, the Indians played the Royals in Kansas City. In the bottom of the ninth, the game was tied with one out and Royal shortstop Angel Berroa was perched on second. Paul Phillips lifted a routine fly to center; with one more out, the game would head into extra innings. Indian outfielder Grady Sizemore moved under the ball to make the catch. But then Sizemore lost the ball in the sun and dropped it. He stared at it briefly as it sat in the deep green, sun-soaked Kansas City outfield grass. Meanwhile, Berroa scored unchallenged and a four-game Indian winning streak ended. (Ironically, Sizemore would be awarded Gold Gloves in 2007 and 2008.)

Now Cleveland seemed haunted by history. The Indians lost six of their last seven, and the White Sox were American League Central Division champions. The Sox spent every day of the 2005 season in first place and ended up with 99 wins. Despite going 38-18 during the last two months of the season, the Indians were shut out of the playoffs. They would later blow a World Series to the Cubs in 2016 after taking a three-games-to-one advantage.

The White Sox were on their way to their first world championship in 88 years, even though, one more time, they would be accused of cheating.

With a fist pump, Paul Konerko celebrates his seventh-inning, two-out grand slam in game two of the 2005 World Series. In what can be described as one of the most exciting moments in team history, Konerko ripped into a Chad Qualls fastball that tailed back over the plate. One fan sitting behind the Sox dugout held up a small cardboard sign reading, "I've waited 92 years for this." A statue of Konerko with raised hand now sits on the outfield concourse at Guaranteed Rate Field. (Ron Vesely/Chicago White Sox.)

A nervous Mark Buehrle is making his way from the bullpen to secure the last out of game three of the 2005 World Series. It was the first relief appearance for Buehrle in five seasons, and he was the ninth pitcher the White Sox used in a 14-inning, 5:41 contest. He induced Adam Everett to pop out to shortstop Juan Uribe to close out a 7-5 win. This was quite a feat for Buehrle after throwing seven innings in game two only two days earlier and having imbibed a few beers in the bullpen. (Ron Vesely/Chicago White Sox.)

Manager Ozzie Guillen and franchise CEO Jerry Reinsdorf conduct a high-level confab at the end of the White Sox dugout. Guillen came to the White Sox first as a player in December 1984. He was the cornerstone of a trade involving 1983 Cy Young Award winner LaMarr Hoyt. Initial reaction was not good because of Hoyt's popularity. But Guillen was named American League Rookie of the Year in 1985, won a Gold Glove in 1990, and was named to three All-Star teams. He became the first Chicago baseball manager to win a World Series since 1917. (Ron Vesely/Chicago White Sox.)

Left-hander Mark Buehrle will always be remembered by White Sox fans for his consistency and professionalism. He threw two no-hitters during his 214-win career. On April 18, 2007, Buerhle no-hit the Texas Rangers 6-0. He allowed one base runner when he walked Sammy Sosa in the fifth. Buerhle then picked Sosa off, leaving the Rangers with only 26 official at-bats for the game. A little over two years later, on July 23, 2009, Buehrle picked up his perfect game against the Tampa Bay Rays, who gave him an ovation from their dugout steps. Both no-hitters were completed in two hours and three minutes, a typical efficient Buehrle start. (Ron Vesely/Chicago White Sox.)

This is another time A.J. Pierzynski showed his competitiveness. In the September 30, 2008, "Blackout Game" to determine the winner of the American League Central, the White Sox played the Twins at home. With one out in the top of the fifth, Twins DH Michael Cuddyer stood on third. Brendan Harris lifted a fly to shallow center. Ken Griffey Jr. camped under the ball, neatly positioned himself and uncorked a perfect two-hop throw to the plate. Doing a great job of blocking the plate, Pierzynski helped complete an inning-ending double play. The White Sox won the game 1-0 and the division title on the strength of a Jim Thome home run that is still circling the earth somewhere. (Ron Vesely/Chicago White Sox.)

In the beginning of his career, Joe Crede's swing didn't always look this good. But at a game in late September 2005, the author heard one fan ask, "What has gotten into Joe Crede?" That game Crede homered and knocked a line shot single to left. The swing looked just fine. Crede came through with a variety of dramatic hits in 2005, including a walk-off homer against the surging Indians in late September. His defensive play during the World Series reminded many fans of Hall of Fame third baseman Brooks Robinson. Robinson put on a defensive show in the 1970 World Series against the Reds. Crede did the same in the 2005 World Series against the Astros. (Ron Vesely/Chicago White Sox.)

One of the more fiery and competitive White Sox players, Aaron Rowand is shown here hustling one out between second and third. Rowand roamed center field and did anything to snag a drive. He leapt, he ran, he dove. He was disappointed to hear he was traded to the Phillies for Jim Thome after the 2005 season. Some fans thought the trade harmed the chemistry of the team. (Ron Vesely/Chicago White Sox.)

White Sox CEO Jerry Reinsdorf, as with Charles Comiskey, had public image problems. Some fans simply regarded him as cheap. However, the author knows of at least two stories that demonstrate Reinsdorf's generosity. Under Reinsdorf, the White Sox have been the first Chicago baseball team to win a division title, the first Chicago baseball team to draw over two million in a season, and the first Chicago baseball team to win a World Series in 88 years. Technically not the owner, Reinsdorf has run the franchise longer than any other executive or owner in team history. (Ron Vesely/Chicago White Sox.)

A.J. Pierzynski was not a popular player during his major-league career. Most wouldn't have liked him unless he was a teammate. In one of the most dramatic wins against the Dodgers, on June 18, 2005, Pierzynski hit an opposite-field home run to win the game in the ninth. It was one of those close games the White Sox should not have won, as they managed only three hits in the first eight innings. Pierzynski became involved in one of the most controversial plays during the 2005 postseason—or any postseason. Did Josh Paul really trap that third strike? Does it really matter? (Ron Vesely/Chicago White Sox.)

The frustration finally ends. On October 26, 2005, the World Series trophy is presented to the Chicago White Sox after their sweep of the Houston Astros. From left to right are White Sox CEO Jerry Reinsdorf, Major League Baseball commissioner Bud Selig, Sox general manager Ken Williams, and field manager Ozzie Guillen. All the games in the Series were decided by either one or two runs. (Ron Vesely/Chicago White Sox.)

Eric Zorn is a longtime columnist for the *Chicago Tribune* and a lifetime Cubs fan. Zorn's August 22, 2005, column dreamed of a late-season White Sox collapse that would lead to the team failing to make the playoffs with the Cleveland Indians bearing down on Zorn's hated White Sox. Although 2005 led to disappointment for Zorn, he still recalls the column with fondness. In late 2018, Zorn described the column to the author as "my absolute favorite memory of the 2005 White Sox season—the opportunity to write this column, which went viral, was priceless." Zorn rationalized his ill will because of his belief in the horrible treatment of Cubs fans by their South Side counterparts. However, in early 2019, he stated that he had "converted to White Sox fandom," and that he "just had it with the Cubs." (Courtesy of Eric Zorn.)

Arguably one of the most popular of all White Sox players, Paul Konerko gestures a good-bye to fans during his last major-league appearance on September 28, 2014. The chant "Paulie, Paulie," was often heard when he was at the plate. In a press conference after his final game, Konerko said he was surprised to look into the stands to see tears. From the beginning, he was seen as a team leader and positive role model. Konerko was one of those rare players who spent almost his entire career with one team. He hit 439 homers in that career, but many say he won't make it into the Hall of Fame. Regardless, Konerko will be remembered by White Sox fans for decades to come. (Ron Vesely/Chicago White Sox.)

110 OVERCOMING HISTORY

8

SHOELESS JOE JACKSON

Historically, one baseball name evokes powerful emotions like no other: Shoeless Joe Jackson. His stats, starting with his third-best .356 lifetime average, are well known. His best overall year was 1920, when he hit 12 home runs, drove in 121, and had 218 hits including 20 triples. But his overall accomplishments are not at issue. What matters most and riles many is what he did in the eight games of the 1919 World Series.

Did Jackson, despite his .375 Series average, do his best to throw the Series to the Reds? Did he hide behind his lack of education to deny his wrongdoing? Did he betray himself, his fans, and his team? Some claim his banishment from baseball was justified and should not be lifted even nearly 70 years after his death.

In a story he told to journalist Furman Bisher in 1949, Jackson defended his play and reputation in several ways.

First, he pointed out his Series stats, both defensive and offensive. He proudly spoke of his .375 Series average and that he had one hit taken away from him when an official scorer changed the hit to an error. In addition to playing errorless ball, he stated that he never let a runner take an extra base and denied that he compromised himself by playing out of position.

"That's my record in the Series," Jackson told Bisher, "and I was responsible only for Joe Jackson." This statement was an effort to isolate himself from the others, the guilty others.

Jackson also told a story of being directly approached by a gambler before the Series in a 16th-floor hotel room. Jackson directly quoted himself as saying to the gambler, "Why you cheap so-and-so! Either me or you—one of us is going out that window."

According to Jackson, the gambler was able to get away before Jackson could attack him. Jackson maintained that baseball journalist Hugh Fullerton witnessed the confrontation, but by the time Jackson told this story in 1949, Fullerton had died and couldn't collaborate the account. He also said Fullerton had offered to testify in the 1921 trial, but did not, and Jackson was not clear about why.

Finally, Jackson strongly denied the "Say it ain't so, Joe" story about a young boy confronting him as he exited the grand jury courtroom in 1920. Jackson accused Charley Owens of the *Chicago Daily News* of making it up, even though "there wasn't a bit of truth in it." Of course, it would have been hard for Jackson to defend his innocence if he had admitted to the hero-worshipping fan that it was so. This was especially true when he went to court to sue Charles Comiskey and the White Sox in 1924.

Jackson summed up his case by saying, "I can say my conscience is clear and that I'll stand on my record in that World Series."

In Greenville, South Carolina, in 2006, the last home of Joe Jackson was moved across the street from Fluor Field, a minor-league facility in the Boston Red Sox system. The modest but smart-looking redbrick structure serves as a museum honoring Jackson. Even 100 years after the infamous World Series, Joe Jackson is still remembered and admired, especially in his home state.

If a trial were held today, would Joe Jackson be convicted of throwing the 1919 World Series? No matter the verdict, the debate about Shoeless Joe will continue. The case against him is not all that strong even though some still think he betrayed major-league baseball and its fans. He did take the $5,000, didn't he?

What can be said is that only a serious injury would have prevented Joe Jackson from finishing his career with 3,000 hits. His legacy as one of baseball's greatest hitters would only have been enhanced. And no doubt he would have made additional contributions to baseball after his playing days were done.

Shoeless Joe Jackson was sometimes attacked because some of his accounts were inconsistent. But many people are not used to giving public testimony, and a lack of consistency does not necessarily make them a liar.

Historically, the Black Sox scandal still hangs over Major League Baseball and the Chicago White Sox. One way to make peace with the past is to make peace with the memory of Shoeless Joe Jackson. Forgive him any sins he may or may not have committed. Say it ain't so, and enshrine Shoeless Joe Jackson into the Baseball Hall of Fame.

JOSEPH JEFFERSON JACKSON
"SHOELESS JOE"

PHILADELPHIA ATHLETICS 1908 - 1909
CLEVELAND NAPS 1910-1915
CHICAGO WHITE SOX 1915-1920

POSITION-LEFT FIELD THREW RIGHT BATTED LEFT

1911 HIGHEST BATTING AVERAGE EVER BY A ROOKIE .408
1912 LED AMERICAN LEAGUE IN TRIPLES
1913 LED AL IN HITS SLUGGING PERCENTAGE .551
1917 LED CHICAGO WHITE SOX TO WORLD SERIES
VICTORY AGAINST NEW YORK GIANTS
1919 WORLD SERIES BATTING AVERAGE .375
THIRD HIGHEST CAREER BATTING AVERAGE
IN BASEBALL HISTORY .356

This plaque hangs at the Shoeless Joe Jackson Museum in his hometown of Greenville, South Carolina. It symbolizes the hope that a similar plaque will eventually be exhibited at the Baseball Hall of Fame. Many believe Jackson's career and efforts in the 1919 World Series merit an induction. The strongest argument centers around his .356 lifetime batting average. At this point, Major League Baseball has not forgiven Jackson for his alleged involvement in the Black Sox scandal, and he remains barred from the hall. After a century, his name still stirs strong emotions. Many are devoted to his memory, and others are extremely hostile for his perceived betrayal. (Courtesy of the Shoeless Joe Jackson Museum.)

Bobby Richardson, a fellow South Carolina native, spent his entire 12-year career with the New York Yankees. Playing second base, Richardson won four Gold Gloves. In 1962, in the seventh game of the World Series, the Yankees led the San Francisco Giants 1-0 in the bottom of the ninth. The Giants had men on second and third with two out. With the right-handed starter Ralph Terry on the mound, the Yankees chose to pitch to the left-handed power-hitting Willie McCovey, even with right-handed batter Orlando Cepeda in the on-deck circle. On a full-count pitch, McCovey hit a vicious line drive right into the glove of Richardson, who made the catch chest-high to end the game and the series. Richardson is pictured speaking at the opening of the Shoeless Joe Jackson Museum. Like so many others, he is attracted to the Joe Jackson persona. (Courtesy of the Shoeless Joe Jackson Museum.)

Baseball fan Dan Roberts, dressed in turn-of-the-century uniform, sits in front of the door with the address of the Shoeless Joe Jackson Museum. Honoring Jackson's lifetime batting average, the address assigned to the museum is 356 Field Street. The bat resembles Jackson's bat known as "Black Betsy." (Courtesy of Shoeless Joe Jackson Museum.)

Fluor Field at the West End is the home of the single-A minor affiliate of the Boston Red Sox. In this image, Shoeless Joe dominates the center of the scoreboard. The stadium is across the street from the Shoeless Joe Jackson Museum. (Courtesy of Shoeless Joe Jackson Museum.)

This 1917 uniform, which symbolically supports the World War I troops, hangs in the Shoeless Joe Jackson Museum. As more players were called into service in 1918, Major League Baseball faced an economic and competitive crisis. If the war dragged on, it was feared baseball operations would have to cease. Thankfully, for the troops and baseball, the war ended in late 1918. Then, after 1919, Major League Baseball faced an even deeper crisis. It would cost Joe Jackson his career and a good deal of his reputation. (Courtesy of the Shoeless Joe Jackson Museum)

A group of fans sitting right outside the Shoeless Joe Jackson Museum sing "Take Me Out to the Ball Game." It has been a long-standing tradition to sing the song during the seventh-inning stretch. In the late 1970s, White Sox owner Bill Veeck came up with an idea. Why not have a lousy singer lead the fans? White Sox announcer Harry Caray, who could not carry any tune, was enlisted to become the lead singer. He took the practice over to the North Side when he became the Cubs play-by-play announcer in 1982. After Caray's death in 1998, the Cubs have used a host of celebrities to do the lead singing honors. (Courtesy of the Shoeless Joe Jackson Museum.)

This long line of fans outside the Shoeless Joe Jackson Museum is an indication of the long-lasting interest in Jackson. One hundred years after the scandal and decades after Jackson's passing, the debate about and fascination with the central figure in the 1919 World Series has not dampened. One thing cannot be debated: The mere mention of Joe Jackson's name stirs strong emotions, whether it be anger, bitterness, sorrow, or awe over his ability as a hitter. (Courtesy of Shoeless Joe Jackson Museum.)

The Post-Journal

POST - 1901
JOURNAL - 1826

Telephone 7-111

Jamestown Newspaper Corp.
JAMESTOWN, NEW YORK

--COPY--

Mr. A.B. Chandler,
Commissioner,
Cincinnati, Ohio

Dear Mr. Chandler:

I recall the Shoeless Joe Jackson case well, and have always been amazed at the chain of conflicting stories that have been printed, broadcast and passed from mouth-to-mouth down through the years following the ill-famous "Black Sox" scandal.

Believing Jackson was not in on any deal, I strongly urge he be reinstated to the good graces of baseball. If ever there was a mis-carriage of justice, this is one.

Sincerely,
Frank Hyde, Sports Editor

This undated and short letter makes the case for Major League Baseball to reinstate Joe Jackson. It is not known if letter writer Frank Hyde ever received an answer, but Commissioner Chandler took no action on behalf of Jackson.

JIM CROUCH
PUBLICITY
55 WEST 83rd ST.
NEW YORK 24, N.Y.

March 3, 1948.

Mr. Joseph Jackson
Jackson's Package Shop,
West Greenville,
South Carolina.

Dear Joe:

You will recall me as the Jim Crouch who some ten or 15 years ago wrote a column in The Greenville, South Carolina, PIEDMONT, and often mentioned you in my daily piece. Not only that but I had many pleasant visits with you at your barbecue stand on the outskirts of Greenville where we chatted pleasantly of your baseball career.

The point of this letter is that I want to prepare a piece for a national magazine with a view to not only showing you as the greatest natural baseball player of all time but to also show that your name should be cleared of all guilt in the Chicago White Sox affair. I would call the piece: "NATURAL DOUBT ABOUT A NATURAL HITTER."

What I want you to do is to get your wife to mail to me insured your scrapbooks to get some material from and I will study them and return them the minute I have learned some facts I wish from them. I will give you my word of honor you shall receive them back in the same good shape you send them to me.

It has been a long time since I saw you and hope that all is well with you and yours. I guess you are no longer active in Mill baseball as a player-- but wouldn't doubt it if you are still knocking them over the fence.

Please let me hear from me as soon as possible and try to send your scrap books along to me at the above address at the same time.

I have enclosed a short history of my life and words of my trustworthiness are included. Also on the back of this letter are things famous columnists have quoted from me.

Best to all our friends there.

Sincerely,

Jim Crouch.
Jim Crouch.

Enclosed Jim Crouch life business history.

P.S.: Joe, if I am able to sell this piece-- as I am sure I will you will be cut in for from 30% to 40% of the check-- what ever you think is fair. I will have to look over a lot of baseball records besides your scrapbooks. Jim Crouch. *Jim Crouch*

In this rather strange letter from sports journalist Jim Crouch, an attempt at checkbook journalism was made. Many things have been said about Joe Jackson, but it has not been alleged that he tried to directly make money from the 1919 affair.

Joe Jackson shows off his toothy grin in much happier times. Jackson strongly denied that any disillusioned young boy approached him outside the courthouse. One short film clip of the scene does not show a boy by Jackson. However, a man named Roland Gehre eventually stepped forward and said he was the young boy. After Gehre died in 1989, his son Steve and his widow, Alma, still vouched for his honesty. Reportedly, some young fans did confront White Sox players, but that was at the ballpark, not the courthouse. The fans got no response from the players. Regardless, there was plenty of disillusionment, and Jackson felt dogged by the story, which just adds to the confusion of the 1919 scandal.

Joe Jackson ran a liquor store in his later years. The most famous story concerning the store was when Ty Cobb stopped in to make a purchase. Cobb recognized Jackson and told him what a great swing Jackson had. Jackson was somewhat surprised that Cobb acknowledged him since he had begun to think he didn't matter to fans or anyone connected to baseball anymore.

These mortgage statements were signed by Joe's brother Dave because of Joe's illiteracy. In a way, the inability to read and write would haunt Jackson as much as the 1919 scandal did.

THE 1919 BLACK SOX SCANDAL

Joe Jackson's living room now has photographs and mementos highlighting his career and personal life. Above the curtains is a sample of his signature. For a great deal of his life, the illiterate Jackson could not sign legal documents, which included his baseball contracts. The research room is named in honor of Gene Carney, the author of *Burying the Black Sox: How Baseball's Cover-Up of the 1919 World Series Fix Almost Succeeded*. Carney put a great deal of blame for the culture of gambling in baseball on Comiskey and the Major League Baseball establishment. Others claim that Comiskey was simply betrayed by his backstabbing players. (Courtesy of Shoeless Joe Jackson Museum.)

The Jackson master bedroom is where Jackson died of a heart attack at age 64. The green seat and the bricks below are from old Comiskey Park. The park, known for its stately windows and majestic appearance, was the home of the White Sox from 1910 to 1990. The replacement stadium, now known as Guaranteed Rate Field, was built across the street and is almost 30 years old at this writing. (Courtesy of the Shoeless Joe Jackson Museum.)

This modest but comfy-looking Greenville, South Carolina, brick home was where Shoeless Joe Jackson lived later in life and where he died in 1951. Presently, the home is the site of a museum that honors and recalls Jackson's career. The residents of Greenville are proud of Jackson, and this quote is listed on the front page of the Jackson Museum website: "In Greenville, South Carolina, there is no doubt that the legacy of Shoeless Joe Jackson is safe at home. His home." His home was moved to this site in 2006. (Courtesy of Shoeless Joe Jackson Museum.)

These "footsteps" lead to the entrance of the Shoeless Joe Jackson Museum. Many believe that Jackson should be reinstated into Major League Baseball and inducted into the Baseball Hall of Fame. Was Jackson guilty of throwing the 1919 World Series? History still hasn't decided that. The author believes that, after a century, it is time to make peace with Joe Jackson. It is time to recognize what kind of baseball player he was and could have been. It is time to recognize that he paid for whatever sins he may or may not have committed. It is time to place Shoeless Joe Jackson in the Hall of Fame. (Courtesy of the Shoeless Joe Jackson Museum.)

DISCOVER THOUSANDS OF LOCAL HISTORY BOOKS FEATURING MILLIONS OF VINTAGE IMAGES

Arcadia Publishing, the leading local history publisher in the United States, is committed to making history accessible and meaningful through publishing books that celebrate and preserve the heritage of America's people and places.

Find more books like this at
www.arcadiapublishing.com

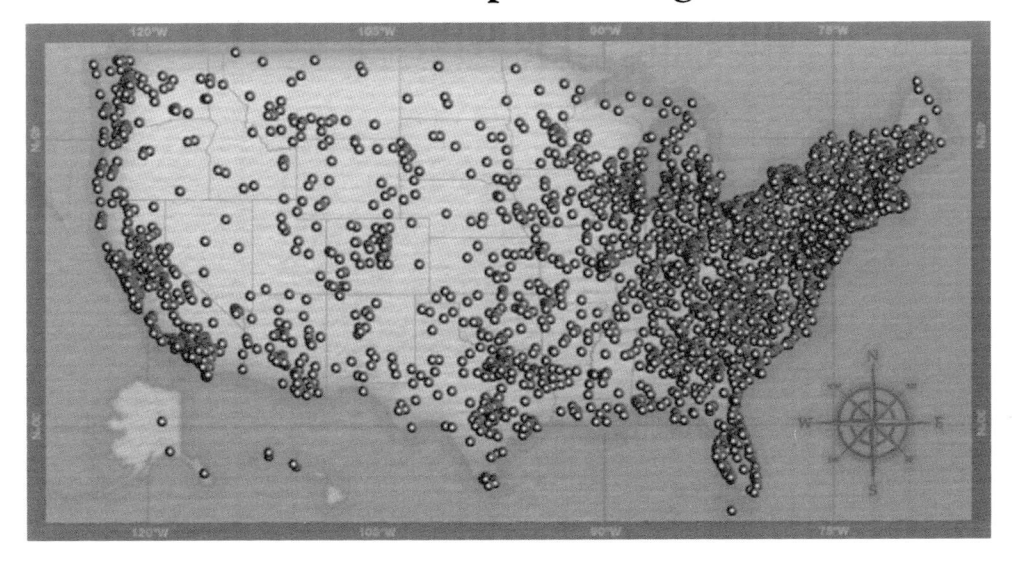

Search for your hometown history, your old stomping grounds, and even your favorite sports team.

Consistent with our mission to preserve history on a local level, this book was printed in South Carolina on American-made paper and manufactured entirely in the United States. Products carrying the accredited Forest Stewardship Council (FSC) label are printed on 100 percent FSC-certified paper.

MADE IN THE USA